INTERPRETING DATA: A GUIDE TO UNDERSTANDING RESEARCH

PETER M. NARDI

Pitzer College

D1359851

Boston New York San Francisco
Mexico City Montreal Toronto London Madrid Munich Paris
Hong Kong Singapore Tokyo Cape Town Sydney

Senior Series Editor: *Jeff Lasser*
Editorial Assistant: *Heather McNally*
Senior Marketing Manager: *Kelly May*
Composition and Prepress Buyer: *Linda Cox*
Manufacturing Buyer: *JoAnne Sweeney*
Editorial-Production Coordinator: *Mary Beth Finch*
Electronic Composition: *Publishers' Design and Production Services, Inc.*

For related titles and support materials, visit our online catalog at
www.ablongman.com

Between the time Website information is gathered and then published,
it is not unusual for some sites to have closed. Also, the transcription of
URLs can result in unintended typographical errors. The publisher
would appreciate notification where these errors pccir so that they may
be corrected in subsequent editions.

Library of Congress Cataloging-in-Pubilcation Data

Nardi, Peter M.
   Interpreting data : a guide to understanding research / Peter M. Nardi.
     p. cm.
  ISBN 0-205-43919-5 (paperback)
    1. Social sciences—Statistical methods. 2. Social surveys.
   3. Social Sciences—Research—Methodology. I. Title

HA29.N34 2006
001.4'22—dc22

                                        2004060201

Printed in the United States of America

10 9 8 7 6 5 4 3 2 1 10 09 08 07 06 05

Credits appear beginning on page 115, which should be considered an
extension of this copyright page

CONTENTS

PREFACE

Welcome to *Interpreting Data: A Guide to Understanding Research* with *Research Navigator™*.

This text is accompanied by our *Research Navigator Guide* that will help you search for and retrieve articles from hundreds of scholarly journals, popular magazines, and newspapers where data from scientific studies is published. You can use the search engines in *Research Navigator™* to find the articles you want from any computer with an Internet connection. A six-month subscription to *Research Navigator™* is free with every new copy of *Interpreting Data*. *Research Navigator™* includes two sources of scientific data discussed in this text:

Scholarly Articles.

EBSCO's *ContentSelect* Academic Journal Database is an archive of thousands of articles from scholarly, peer-reviewed journals, organized by academic discipline. These articles provide specialized knowledge and information on specific research topics, and follow strict scientific guidelines. You can search for articles in *ContentSelect* by using the title, author, subject, or the unique Article Number [AN] assigned to each article. **Many of the examples and exercises in this text are taken from articles available through *ContentSelect*.**

Popular Publications.

Newspapers and magazines are issues in regular installments (daily, weekly or monthly), and provide information for a general reading audience. *ContentSelect* includes a "General Interest" subject database that includes articles from publications such as *Newsweek*, the *Christian Science Monitor*, and *USA Today Magazine*. *Research Navigator™* also includes a "Search by Subject" archive of one full year of the New York *Times*.

In addition, *Research Navigator™* includes extensive online help on:

- Starting the research process
- Finding and evaluating sources
- Citing sources
- Conducting Internet research
- Using your library
- Starting to write

To gain access to *Research Navigator*™, go to www.researchnavigator.com

Register using the access code on the inside front cover of the *Research Navigator Guide,* and set up your free subscription by following the screen prompts.

ACKNOWLEDGMENTS

This book is the outcome of nearly 30 years of teaching quantitative research methods and statistics to undergraduates ot Pitzer College, a member of the Claremont Colleges. By working at the interpretation of statistics, students came to understand how best to do research and analyze data. Their patience, curiosity, and perseverance contributed to the development of this book.

This book also owes its existence to my editor Jeff Lasser and his staff for their continuing commitment to my ideas and for their expert supervision of its production.

Finally, and most importantly, this book is only possible because of Jeff Chemin, who has all the data he needs to know why. This one is also for you.

INTRODUCTION

To read graphs and tables of numbers found in newspaper and magazine articles, to interpret statistics in scholarly and scientific publications, and to understand the output from statistical software are important skills in today's data-oriented world. For many people, however, interpreting data is like learning a foreign language and requires practice and experience with real situations.

THE GOALS

Interpreting Data: A Guide to Understanding Research is designed to assist in the interpretation of basic statistics, tables, and graphs that are used regularly in popular and academic writing. It is written in non-technical everyday language and designed to be a supplementary text for people who want a quick understanding of how to read data or who are learning statistics from a standard research methods or statistical textbook. The book is neither a how-to book showing the way to calculate statistics nor a guide to using statistical software. However, it does present SPSS output, data, and statistics from actual academic publications, and tables of numbers and charts from everyday sources, such as public opinion polls and survey research reports. The goal is to be able to read these figures and tables and to make intelligent interpretations.

Although the material can be read in any order, the first few chapters provide good beginning steps in interpreting tables of data and doing descriptive statistical analyses. Then the chapters introduce the more advanced statistical techniques and their meanings. The information in *Interpreting Data* is enhanced by reading along with a statistics textbook, which can clarify many concepts. The Internet could also be searched for a variety of on-line statistics, methods books, and glossaries.

1

THE FORMAT

Each chapter introduces a statistic, table, graph, or figure by

a. first providing a definition of it,
b. describing under what conditions or assumptions it should and should not be used,
c. illustrating its use three ways: in a popular publication (if available), an academic article, and SPSS output, and
d. interpreting the meaning of the statistic, table, or graph.

The *interpretation* of each statistic, table, or graph in turn involves:

a. first identifying the variables and why this statistic, table, or graph was used,
b. describing what is going on in the table and with any statistics or graphs,
c. putting a conclusion into everyday language, and
d. explaining or hypothesizing the reasons for the results found

In addition, each chapter incorporates real examples as *exercises* to put into practice what was just learned. These exercises are placed throughout a chapter in boxes as a way of measuring learning progress at various points.

DEFINITIONS

Understanding the material requires familiarity with specific terms and concepts that are routinely taught in research methods and statistics classes. For those readers who need a review and for those who have not yet studied research methods and statistics, here is a glossary of key words.

■ **Variables** are measurable concepts that can have different values. These values *vary* across the sample under study; for example, the variable "Religion" has several possible values: Catholic, Buddhist, Jewish, Protestant, Muslim, and None. Variables measure behaviors, attitudes, opinions, and demographic characteristics describing the participants (such as age, race/ethnicity, and gender).

■ **Values** are the categories used to represent a concept's variability. The variable "political party" can have such categories as "Republican," "Democrat," "Conservative," "Labor," or whatever is appropriate for a particular sample. An easy way to distinguish the *variables* from the *values* is to remember that the survey question is often the variable and the answers are typically the values.

■ **Independent Variables** are those concepts used to explain or predict another variable. A study might use "ethnicity/race" to predict or explain "voting behavior." In this case, "ethnicity/race" is the independent variable that occurs or exists in time before the occurrence of voting.

■ **Dependent Variables** are those concepts that depend on the other variables for their occurrence. They contain the outcomes or predicted values that are explained by the independent variables. In the previous example, "voting behavior" would be the outcome dependent on, or maybe caused by, race/ethnicity.

■ **Nominal Measured Variables** are categories or characteristics that have no numerical or ordered meaning. A variable called "type of car owned" can take on many values including "Honda," "Chevrolet," "Volkswagen," and so on. These nominal categories are in no particular order and have no mathematical or numerical properties. They are simply names used to measure the "car owned" variable. A numeral could be assigned to each answer for ease in coding the answers for computer analysis, but the numeral assigned is arbitrary and does not have any mathematical properties: "Honda" could be a 1, or it could be a 3 or 12. There is no order and an answer assigned a 4 is not twice that of one assigned a 2.

■ **Ordinal Measured Variables**, on the other hand, are named categories that have some order to them. Because of this order, a numeral can be assigned to each category to designate the order. For example, a survey question might ask how often in the past month you ate in a restaurant. The variable is "frequency of eating in a restaurant" and the values or answers are "Frequently," "Sometimes," and "Never." The "Frequently" category can be assigned a 1, "Sometimes" given a 2, and "Never" a 3. They are in order of frequency so you cannot just give "Frequently" a 2 and then "Sometimes" a 3 and "Never" a 1. Where you start labeling with a numeral is often arbitrary, but once you start, you have to continue numbering the categories in order. So you could say that "Never" is a 1, then "Sometimes" would have to be a 2, and "Frequently" a 3. The best-sellers book listings or the Top 40 ranking of CDs sold are examples of ordinal measured variables.

■ **Interval** and **Ratio Measured Variables** have mathematical and numbered properties. The values are actual measured intervals using some counting system, such as inches for height, pounds for weight, or years for age. The only difference between true interval measures and ratio ones is the presence of an absolute zero for ratio variables. This means that you cannot have negative numbers: There is no such thing as -50 pounds, or -2 years of age. Having an absolute zero allows us to say that someone ten years of age is twice as old (a ratio) as a five year old. With interval level variables, zero can be an actual answer, as with temperature, so you cannot say that 20 degrees is twice as warm as 10 degrees. Ratio measures are the only variables that have mathematical properties of addition, subtraction, multiplication, and division, and they are preferred for many of the more advanced statistical analyses. But for all practical purposes, ratio and interval measures can be treated the same way; for simplicity, these measures will be designated as interval/ratio throughout the book. Some ordinal measures, such as Likert scales which tend to range from Strongly Agree to Strongly Disagree answers, as well as dichotomies (two value variables, like True/False or Male/Female) have equal appearing intervals and are often treated as if they were interval/ratio measures.

- A **Hypothesis** is an untested statement about the relationship between two or more variables. These can be derived from theories, hunches, observation, or previous research. Many times they are stated in the *null* form, such as "There is no relationship between attitudes toward capital punishment and educational level."

- A **Population** is the total collection of units or elements you want to analyze. It depends on the availability of a list of all possible elements. For example, a study of the entire population of your hometown requires a list of all names. The characteristics of the population are called the *parameters.*

- A **Sample** is what is more likely to be studied than a population, especially if the population is very large. A sample is composed of a subset of the elements or units of a population, ideally selected using the principles of *random selection* in which every element in the population has an equal chance of being selected. If this is the case, then inferences about the population can be made from the values of the sample's variables. The data used to describe the sample's characteristics are called *descriptive statistics* and data for making estimates about the population are called *inferential statistics.*

- **Generalizability** is the ability to make accurate inferences and descriptions about the population from the sample statistics. However, if true random sampling did not occur and the sample was based on non-probability sampling techniques, such as convenience, purposive, quota, or snowball sampling, you may be limited to making conclusions only about the sample.

- **Sampling error** is the difference between the information gathered from the sample (the statistics) and the true population parameters. The goal is to limit the amount of error in order to make more accurate predictions and explanations of the relationships in the population studied. Most public opinion polls report a sampling error when presenting the results, such as "plus or minus 4.5 percentage points."

- **Significance Level** (p value) is the probability of obtaining a particular statistic by chance. All statistics have two components: the value of the calculation derived from a mathematical formula and the odds of obtaining that value by chance. This is determined by various models of probability, such as the normal bell-shaped curve. For example, a chi-square value might be 3.45 and its significance level is stated as .024. These results would be represented as $\chi = 3.45$, $p < .05$ and tell us that the probability of getting this chi-square value of 3.45 by chance is less than 5% or five out of 100. This is the minimal standard set by most social science research. It means that if this analysis were to be done 100 times, five of them would result in this chi-square by chance. If this chance figure is too high, then other minimums can be set, such as .01 or .001. When the probability level is achieved, we can declare a statistically significant finding and reject the null hypothesis. This leads to a conclusion that there is indeed a relationship between the two variables studied. The significance level set is also the probability of making what is called a *Type I error*, rejecting a null hypothesis when there is truly no relationship between the variables. It is the percentage of times out of 100 that you would say there is a finding when in fact there really isn't one.

The references at the end of the book include some additional statistics and research methods texts for further information.

STATISTICAL ANALYSIS DECISION TREE

Central to interpreting statistical information is understanding levels of measurement and the appropriate use of statistical procedures. As a guide to assisting interpretations, Figure 1 presents a "statistical analysis decision tree" providing steps to make the relevant choices.

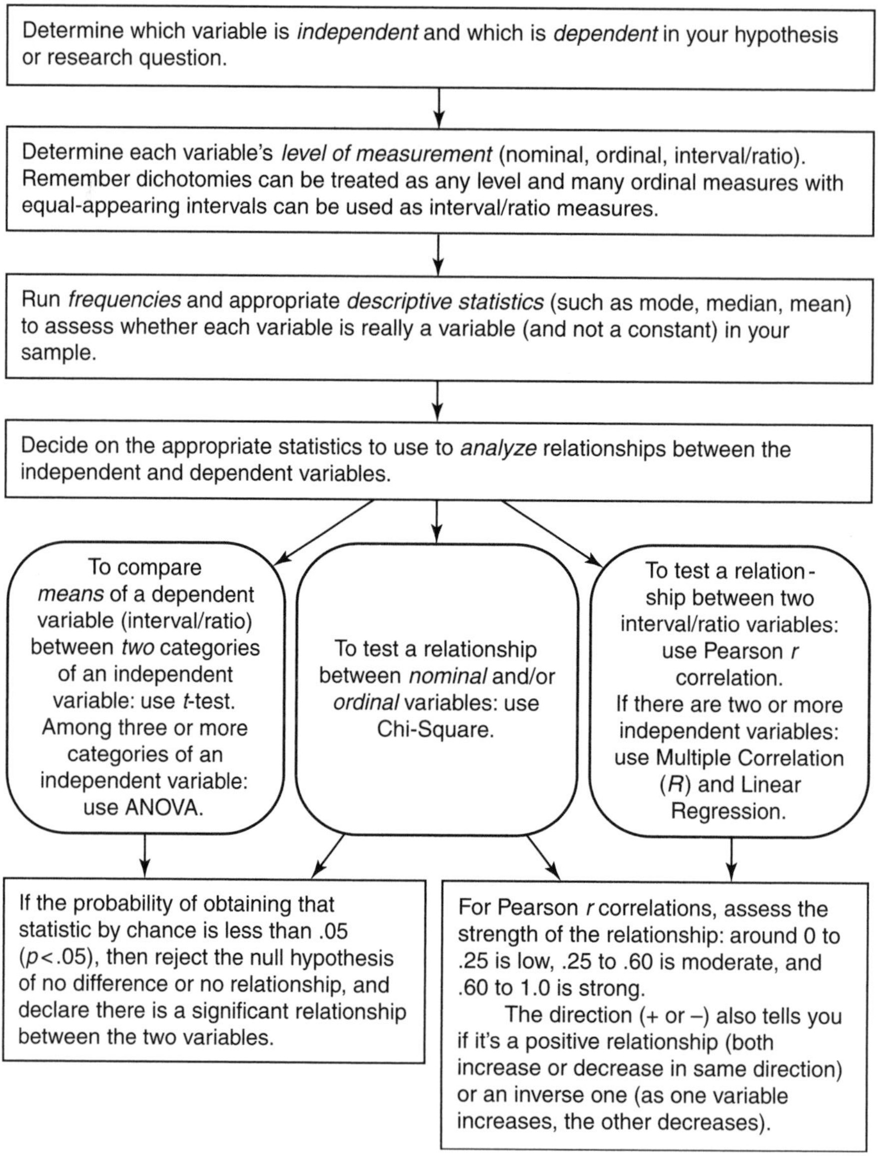

Determine which variable is *independent* and which is *dependent* in your hypothesis or research question.

Determine each variable's *level of measurement* (nominal, ordinal, interval/ratio). Remember dichotomies can be treated as any level and many ordinal measures with equal-appearing intervals can be used as interval/ratio measures.

Run *frequencies* and appropriate *descriptive statistics* (such as mode, median, mean) to assess whether each variable is really a variable (and not a constant) in your sample.

Decide on the appropriate statistics to use to *analyze* relationships between the independent and dependent variables.

To compare *means* of a dependent variable (interval/ratio) between *two* categories of an independent variable: use *t*-test. Among three or more categories of an independent variable: use ANOVA.

To test a relationship between *nominal* and/or *ordinal* variables: use Chi-Square.

To test a relationship between two interval/ratio variables: use Pearson *r* correlation. If there are two or more independent variables: use Multiple Correlation (*R*) and Linear Regression.

If the probability of obtaining that statistic by chance is less than .05 ($p < .05$), then reject the null hypothesis of no difference or no relationship, and declare there is a significant relationship between the two variables.

For Pearson *r* correlations, assess the strength of the relationship: around 0 to .25 is low, .25 to .60 is moderate, and .60 to 1.0 is strong.

The direction (+ or −) also tells you if it's a positive relationship (both increase or decrease in same direction) or an inverse one (as one variable increases, the other decreases).

FIGURE 1   (from *Doing Survey Research: A Guide to Quantitative Methods,* Peter M. Nardi, Allyn & Bacon, 2003)

CHAPTER 1

DESCRIBING DATA

When surveys are returned and data analysis begins, researchers first like to evaluate the items in their questionnaires to determine whether they are indeed variables, that is, that there is sufficient variability to do further data analysis with each one. If an opinion question, for example, resulted in 95% of the respondents "strongly agreeing" to it or if 90% of those responding to the survey are female, then there is usually not much analysis that can be done with those items, unless the sample is very large. There needs to be some variation in the answers given by the respondents for an item to be useful in later data analyses.

Furthermore, an important step in writing up the results of a study is to describe in some detail who completed the surveys (the demographics) along with other general descriptions from the research. This goal of generating descriptive information about the respondents and the key variables is achieved through the use of graphs, descriptive statistics, and frequency tables. This chapter provides information to guide you in interpreting various methods of displaying *univariate* data, that is, one variable at a time.

DEFINITIONS

■ **Measures of Central Tendency** are three measures that summarize where the responses in a distribution for a variable tend to be clustered: the *Mean*, the *Median*, and the *Mode*.

■ The **mean** provides information about the mathematical center of a distribution. It is the sum of all the values in a distribution divided by the number of values.

■ The **median**—like the median that runs down the middle of the highway—is the halfway point in an ordered distribution. It is the value above which half the values fall and below which the other half fall.

■ The **mode** is obtained by finding the most frequently selected value in a distribution of a variable. Do not confuse the mode with the "majority" answer, which is a response that is more than 50%. A majority response is always the mode, but the most frequently occurring value could have been selected by fewer than 50% of the respondents and still qualify as the mode.

- The **standard deviation** tells us how spread out the values in a distribution are. The standard deviation provides a mathematical measure of dispersion or variability. It is somewhat like the average difference from the mean of all the values in a distribution.

- A **percentile** tells you the percentage of responses that fall above and below a particular value point. For example, the median is the 50th percentile because 50% of the responses are above and 50% are below that value.

- A **frequency table** or distribution shows how often each response (a *value*) was given by the respondents to an item (a *variable*). The frequency for each value is listed in absolute raw numbers of occurrence and in percentages relative to the number of total responses (sometimes called the *valid percent*), or relative to the total number of surveys distributed (this figure includes missing answers).

- **Bar charts or graphs** are a visual way of presenting the distribution of a variable. Typically the categories of the variable are placed along the *x*-axis (the horizontal line) and the frequencies (in percent or raw number) are located on the *y*-axis (the vertical line). As the name implies, bar graphs make use of bars that indicate with height the frequency of occurrence of a value relative to the other bars. Sometimes the bars are placed horizontally in which case the categories are on the *y*-axis and the frequency or percentage on the *x*-axis. Length, rather than height, indicates the frequency of occurrence of the values. When making comparisons among charts or graphs, be sure the units of the *y*-axis are similar.

- **Histograms** are similar to bar charts but the bars are adjacent and touching each other to indicate the continuous nature of the measure. The width and height of the bars communicate the number of responses grouped within some designated interval.

- A **frequency polygon** is a line graph that connects the mid-points of each of the bars (or intervals) in the histogram with a line. A common one in the social sciences is the normal or bell-shaped curve. Line graphs are often used to depict changes over time.

- **Pie charts** are a visual way of depicting the occurrence of values of a variable by using the slices of a circle to indicate size or percentage of each value's frequency relative to the other values.

ASSUMPTIONS

The use of various graphs and descriptive statistics is ideally suited for displaying information about one variable at a time (univariate analysis). Which method is used often depends on the variables' levels of measurement.

- *Nominal* measures: Mode, Pie Charts, Bar Graphs
- *Ordinal* measures: Median, Mode, Pie Charts, Bar Graphs
- *Interval/Ratio* measures: Mean, Median, Mode, Standard Deviation, Histograms (for continuous variables), Bar Graphs (for discrete variables), Frequency Lines and Curves, Percentiles

DATA FROM POPULAR PUBLICATIONS

Pie Chart

Each year the U.S. Department of Education through its National Center for Education Statistics reports on a wide range of information about public education. Tables of data are often visually summarized with graphs. Consider the pie chart in Figure 1.1 and see if you can interpret it before proceeding.

Identifying the Variables.   Pie charts are suitable for one variable at a time and, in this case, the graph shows the breakdown of race/ethnicity among public elementary and secondary students during the 2001–2002 school year. A good chart should present an adequate summary in its title as well as the "source" of the data. Race/ethnicity is a nominal level measure since the categories of the variable have no inherent order.

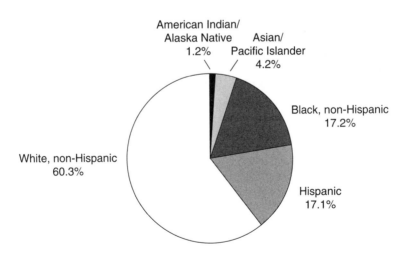

FIGURE 1.1   Percentage of public elementary and secondary students, by race/ethnicity: School year 2001–02

Source: U.S. Department of Education, National Center for Education Statistics, Common Core of Data (CCD), "State Nonfiscal Survey of Public Elementary/Secondary Education," 2001–02.

Interpreting the Table.   Even without looking at the percentages, it is easy to see immediately that the largest sliver of the pie is for White, non-Hispanic, followed by Black, non-Hispanic and then Hispanic students.

A pie chart is a simple and quick visual method of presenting numerical information (in this case, percentages). Many charts do not print the percentages; a frequency table is often better for listing the specific categories along with the exact percentages.

Making Conclusions and Explaining the Results.   As a snapshot of one particular school year, this pie chart quickly shows us the largest racial/ethnic groups in public schools. But not much more can be done with this unless there are some comparable data. For example, do these figures represent increases or decreases in each category from another school year? Or how does the racial/ethnic breakdown compare with private schools? Finally, are these numbers proportionate to the population at large, or are some groups over- or under-represented in public schools?

Bar Graph

An alternative way of depicting frequency distributions is through bar graphs, which are especially useful when several layers of data need to be communicated simultaneously, as the following figure demonstrates. In Figure 1.2 on page 11 both bar graphs and numerical frequencies are presented.

Identifying the Variables.   This figure represents the percentage of high school graduates, 18 to 24 years of age at the time of the survey, and their highest level of educational attainment. It compares those who spoke English only at home and those who spoke other languages. Hence, the variables are "educational attainment" and "language spoken at home." Age is not a variable but a constant, since every one in the sample is in the same age range category. Furthermore, high school completer status is not a variable, since every one is at least a high school graduate.

Interpreting the Table.   Begin with either variable: educational attainment or language at home. Even without looking at the percentages, the length of the bars suggests that most went beyond high school diplomas. The length of the bars for high school are about the same size as "some college" indicating that the percentage currently in or who have had some college is about the same number as graduated from high school. But note that some have attained an Associate's degree and a Bachelor's degree already. If the survey were done with, let's say people in their 40s, what might the bars look like then?

If we are interested in seeing if language at home makes a difference, we would compare the length of the bars within each level of education. No-

Highest educational attainment

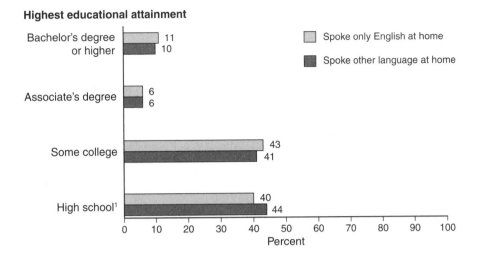

FIGURE 1.2   **Percentage distribution of 18- to 24-year-olds who completed high school, by highest educational attainment and by language characteristics: 1999**

[1]High school completers include those who completed high school by means of an equivalency test such as the GED.

Note: Detail may not sum to totals because of rounding.

Source: U.S. Department of Commerce, Bureau of the Census, Current Population Survey (CPS), October 1999.

tice that they are about the same, suggesting that language at home does not make a difference whether or not the young people received a Bachelor's degree or Associate's degree. Yet, a larger percentage of those who spoke another language at home did not go beyond high school (44%) compared with those who spoke only English at home (40%).

Making Conclusions and Explaining the Results.   We can conclude that slightly more "English speaking only" people have attended college compared with those who also spoke another language at home. The table does not provide an answer why this may be so. A literature review and a look at data from other age ranges might indicate whether this result is a short-term finding (only applicable for 18 to 24 year olds) or something that would change as they get older. Such data raise more questions than they answer, but given the descriptive goals of the table, bar graphs provide a visually clean and quick summary of the information. Note also that the table does not report any tests of significance, so we cannot statistically conclude that

English speaking only people have more education than those who spoke another language at home.

■ ■ ■ ■ ■

BOX 1.1

NOW IT'S YOUR TURN

Here is a chart that appeared in "The Condition of Education 2004" report from the National Center for Education Statistics.

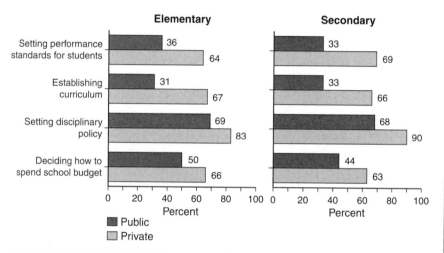

PRINCIPAL INFLUENCE: Percentage of principals who reported that they have a high degree of influence over specific school governance functions, by school level and control: 1999–2000

QUESTIONS TO ANSWER:

1. What are the variables represented in this figure and their levels of measurement (nominal, ordinal, interval/ratio)?
2. Why is a bar graph suitable for these findings?
3. Describe in words what the graph is showing us. Which bars are the longest and shortest? For example, what does the 66 on the last bar on the left tell us in comparison to the 50 right above it?
4. Make a conclusion about the results using everyday language. Are there differences between elementary and secondary school principals? In what areas do public school principals differ from private school ones the most at each level of school?
5. What could be plausible explanations for the results? Are there any theories or previous research that can guide you in interpreting the findings?

Line Graph

It is often better to present data over time with a line graph. The number of legal immigrants admitted into the United States for permanent residence is represented visually in the line graph in Figure 1.3 from the *1998 Statistical Yearbook* as reported in the 2004 "Language Minorities and Their Educational and Labor Market Indicators–Recent Trends," distributed by the National Center for Education Statistics.

Identifying the Variables.   Number of legal immigrants is an interval/ratio variable and year is an ordinal variable. Given the time dimension, a line graph makes the most sense since it visually illustrates continuous changes over the years.

Interpreting the Table.   Immigration increased dramatically for four consecutive years from 1988 through 1991. The numbers declined quite a bit in 1992, although not to the pre-1988 level, then continued decreasing except for a slight increase in 1996. Note that it is not possible to determine the exact numbers for each year. A frequency table could provide this or the numbers could be entered in the figure. The intention of graphs is to give a quick visual summary of the data, not the specific frequencies.

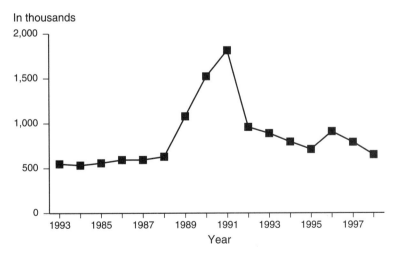

FIGURE 1.3   Number of immigrants to the United States: 1983–98

Note: Graph tick marks represent 100,000 immigrants. "Immigrants" are defined as aliens admitted for permanent legal residence in the United States.

Source: U.S. Department of Justice, Immigration and Naturalization Service. 1998 Statistical Yearbook. Washington, DC: U.S. Government Printing Office.

Making Conclusions and Explaining the Results. Explanations might focus on changes in immigration laws, election year campaigns, or related political events. The chart does not provide an explanation since the purpose is primarily descriptive. The line graph gives a quick visual sense of the changing numbers of legal immigrants to the United States over this 16-year period

Frequency Tables

Frequency tables can easily summarize and compare trends over two different points in time. Table 1.1 presents information from a government report by the National Center for Education Statistics about the changes in homeschooling in the United States.

Identifying the Variables. The variable is "school enrollment status" of kindergarten through twelfth grade students (ages 5 through 17). Several responses were available: "homeschooled only," and "enrolled in school part

TABLE 1.1   Number and percentage distribution of homeschooled students, ages 5 through 17 in kindergarten through 12th grade, by school enrollment status: 1999 and 2003

	Homeschooled students			
School enrollment status	*1999*		*2003*	
	Number	*Percent*	*Number*	*Percent*
Total	850,000	100.0	1,096,000	100.0
Homeschooled only	697,000	82.0	898,000	82.0
Enrolled in school part time	153,000	18.0	198,000	18.0
Enrolled in school for less than 9 hours a week	107,000	12.6	137,000	12.5
Enrolled in school for 9 to 25 hours a week	46,000	5.4	61,000	5.6

Note: Excludes students who were enrolled in public or private school for more than 25 hours per week and students who were homeschooled only because of temporary illness. Detail may not sum to totals because of rounding. Standard errors are available at http://nces.ed.gov/pubsearch/pubinfo.asp?pubid-2004115. There were 50,188,000 5–17-year-old students in kindergarten through 12th grade in 1999, and 50,707,000 in 2003.

Source: U.S. Department of Education, National Center for Education Statistics, Parent Survey of the 1999 National Household Education Surveys Program (NHES); Parent and Family Involvement in Education Survey of the 2003 NHES.

time," which was further broken down into "enrolled in school for less than 9 hours a week" and "enrolled in school for 9 to 25 hours a week." Data for two different years (1999 and 2003) are compared but as the footnote indicates, those students enrolled in schools for more than 25 hours a week or homeschooled due to illness are not included in the table.

This is a nominal measure variable suitable for a frequency table. Raw frequencies and percentages are presented with the totals appearing at the top of the table rather than at the bottom line, as is sometimes done.

Interpreting the Table.   In terms of numbers, there has been a large increase over the four years. Over a million students are homeschooled in 2003 compared with a total of 850,000 in 1999. Of those, 82% were homeschooled only without any hours spent in public or private schools and 18% went to school for some time each week. These percentages are the same in both 1999 and 2003. Although there is a great increase in numbers, in terms of percentages, the proportion of homeschooled children who get only homeschooling remains the same over the years. The 18% who enrolled for some hours per week in schools is broken into 12.5% who attended for less than 9 hours and 5.6% who went for 9 to 15 hours a week in 2003. These percentages are virtually identical to the ones in 1999.

Making Conclusions and Explaining the Results.   There appears to be an increase in homeschooling in the United States but not a shift in the proportion of homeschooled children exclusively staying at home for their education. Although most are homeschooled only, a small percentage do attend schools as well.

Reasons for the increase in overall numbers are not presented in the table. Part of the increase is due to population increases, but it is likely that the numbers have grown even when taking overall population increase into account. Other data from the study not shown in the table suggest that concern about the environment of schools and the desire to provide religious and moral instruction motivate parents to give their children homeschooling.

Other Frequency Tables and Statistics

There are many ways of presenting frequency information and descriptive statistics. Tables 1.2a and 1.2b present other data from the National Center for Education Statistics' Common Core of Data, focusing this time on "Characteristics of the 100 Largest Public Elementary and Secondary School Districts in the United States: 2000–01."

Identifying the Variables.   The variables here are the number of students, teachers, and schools in all districts and in the largest 100. Since these data are actual numbers, the variables are interval/ratio measures. In fact, a ratio is

TABLE 1.2a

	2000–01		
	All districts	*100 largest districts*	*100 largest districts as a percentage of national total*
Students	48,067,834	11,050,902	23.0
Teachers (full-time equivalent)	3,002,947	641,333	21.4
Schools	95,366	15,615	16.4

TABLE 1.2b   Median pupil/teacher ratios in public elementary and secondary schools in the 100 largest school districts in the United States and jurisdictions: School year 2000–01

SCHOOLS	PRIMARY	MIDDLE	HIGH
16.7	16.9	16.6	17.4

then calculated in Table 1.2b to get an indicator of the number of students per teacher in various types of public schools.

Interpreting the Table.   Table 1.2a shows the raw numbers and the percentage of the total numbers that are just in the largest 100 school districts. For example, in school year 2000–2001, there were 95,366 schools in all districts in the U.S., and 15,615 schools in the largest 100 districts: 15,615 divided by 95,366 results in .164, or 16.4%.

Table 1.2b displays the ratio of students to teachers in all districts and broken down (disaggregated) by level of school. It reports the median ratio, that is, the ratio which is at the 50th percentile. For example, half the high schools in the U.S. had fewer than 17.4 students for every teacher during the 2000–2001 school year, and the other half had pupil-teacher ratios greater than 17.4. The ratio is generated by dividing the total number of students by the total number of teachers at each school. All the schools are then ordered with the highest to lowest ratios; the median ratio is the point at which half the schools and their ratios are above and half are below, in this case 17.4.

A mean could have been calculated with the ratios, since the ratios themselves are obviously ratio measures. But the mean is distorted by extreme scores and the reporting agency felt that the median would be a better statistic for these data.

Making Conclusions and Explaining the Results.   We can see that the students in the largest school districts account for 23% of the nation's total enrollment, yet they are attending only 16.4% of the schools and have 21.4% of the teachers. This might suggest larger classes and overcrowding in the largest school districts, that is, larger pupil to teacher ratios.

Table 1.2b does not provide these data disaggregated by school district, although the actual report from which this table was selected gives those numbers. This excerpt does, however, tell us that high schools are more crowded than elementary or middle schools. This makes sense since there are usually fewer secondary schools in the nation's districts than elementary schools.

■ ■ ■ ■ ■

BOX 1.2

NOW IT'S YOUR TURN

Most studies describe their samples by presenting a table summarizing the key demographics of the respondents. Here is a table from a longitudinal welfare reform study conducted by MDRC, a major research organization. In this project, researchers collected data through a structured interview survey and held qualitative semi-structured ethnographic interviews with welfare recipients. The characteristics of both samples are described in this table. (In the table, "UI" refers to unemployment insurance.)

Demographic Characteristics of Survey Sample and Ethnographic Sample

CHARACTERISTIC	SURVEY SAMPLE	ETHNOGRAPHIC SAMPLE
Average age at baseline (years)	30.2	35.8
Racial or ethnic group		
African-American (%)	69.0	45.2
White (%)	2.1	0.0
Hispanic (%)	28.3	54.8
Other (%)	0.7	0.0
Average number of children at baseline	2.7	3.0
Average age of youngest child at baseline (years)	4.9	6.0
Had a high school diploma or GED at baseline (%)	48.9	42.9
Had UI earnings, April 1994 to March 1995 (%)	39.9	n/a
Sample size	581	42

(continued)

BOX 1.2 CONTINUED

Sources: Calculations from the Urban Change Respondent Survey and ethnographic interviews.

Notes: Baseline is May 1995 for the survey sample and December 1997 for the ethnographic sample.

The final interviews were conducted between March and October 2001 for the survey sample and in October 2001 for the ethnographic sample.

Rounding may cause slight discrepancies when adding sums and differences.

Source: Brock, et al. (2004)

QUESTIONS TO ANSWER:

1. What are the variables represented in these figures and their levels of measurement?
2. Why are averages and percentages suitable for these findings?
3. Describe in words what the table is showing us. How different or similar are the two samples?
4. Make a conclusion about the results using everyday language.

SCHOLARLY ARTICLE

When academic articles and scholarly works report the results from quantitative research, most depend on complex statistical analyses. Yet, a verbal description or a table usually provides some information about the sample's characteristics, the distributions of the variables, or other preliminary univariate data analysis.

Frequency Tables

Table 1.3 presents the responses to one question on a sex education survey of parents in Greece. The goal of the research was to assess parental attitudes about the role of the family in their children's sexual development and education.

Identifying the Variables.   The question asks parents to indicate what they see are the sexual development and education problems facing their own children today. The responses fall into 10 specific categories and "Other." Since there is no order to the answers, this item represents a nominal level measure suitable for a frequency table. Given the need to see the percentages for each answer, a table is a better way of presenting the descriptive information than a graph is.

TABLE 1.3   Numbers of answers (*n*) and percentages (%) of parents' answers to the question: *Which problems related to sexual development and sex education of your own children are most serious?*

GROUP OF ANSWERS	*n* (252)	%
Influences from mass media	74	16
Lack of proper information	61	13
Dangers for physical or psychological health	40	8
Lack of sex education in schools	38	8
Negative social influences (drugs, violence, criminality, abnormalities etc.)	36	8
How to become a mature man or a mature woman	31	7
Friendships	29	6
How to speak about sex	24	5
The first sexual experience	22	5
Lack of moral values	21	4
Others	98	20
Total	474	100

Source: Kakavoulis (2001: 171)   [Research Navigator: 4480158]

Interpreting the Table.   Notice that the table indicates 252 respondents (*n*) but a total of 474 responses. Clearly, people were allowed to offer more than one problem that concerns them about their children's sexual development and education. One way to display the findings would be to ask what percentage of the *respondents* chose a particular answer. In this case the table would have to report 74 answers from 252 people: 74/252 = .294 or 29.4% for "influences from the mass media." But it doesn't—instead the table reports the percentage of all *responses* given, that is, 74 out of 474 answers: 74/474 = .156 or 15.6% (in this table rounded off to 16%). In other words, of all the answers provided by the respondents, almost 16% of them focused on the mass media. The other way would have resulted in the statement that 29.4% of the respondents picked mass media as a problem influence on their children's sexual development. The order of the answers would still be the same: The influence of the mass media remains the number one concern among these parents in both methods of presentation.

When the answers to a question are mutually exclusive, that is, only one can be chosen instead of "check all that apply," the percentages for each response is the same when it's based on the number of answers as it is when based on the number of people. Each respondent corresponds with one response then. Here, each respondent could give more than one answer, which explains the difference between the number of people in the survey (*n* = 252) and the number of responses (Total = 474). The label on the table also tells us that the percentages are "of parents' answers."

Making Conclusions and Explaining the Results.   Parents in Greece appear to be concerned about the media's influence on their children's sexual education, along with worrying about children getting the wrong information. Other responses appear to be more equally selected.

Why the parents see problems with the media and incorrect information reaching their children is not explained by this table. With these results, however, a researcher could get comparative data from other countries and then begin to seek some explanations for similarities and differences among cultures. Would responses in your communities be much different?

Descriptive Statistics

In Table 1.4 are some descriptive statistics for a set of measures used in a research project to evaluate the spillover effect of work on the family, that is, how much work life can impinge on family life and create problems at home. This study of 156 dual-earning couples in particular focused on the impact

TABLE 1.4   Descriptive Statistics For Variables Used in the Analysis

	MEN			WOMEN		
VARIABLES	*M*	*SD*	*N*	*M*	*SD*	*N*
Dependent Variable						
Family cohesion	27.79	4.25	150	27.75	4.56	150
Independent Variables						
Emotion-work satisfaction[a]	19.56	3.89	144	20.27	3.16	143
Household-work satisfaction[a]	2.52	.84	153	2.77	.66	146
Work-to-family spillover	13.75	4.07	153	13.93	3.80	150
Job satisfaction[a]	16.66	3.24	153	16.81	3.60	150
Family-friendly benefits satisfaction[a]	4.95	1.49	139	5.01	1.59	130
Job flexibility	20.95	5.33	155	21.27	5.32	152
Average hours worked per week	46.23	13.51	156	36.20	13.35	155
Number of children	1.44	1.46	156	1.56	1.59	156

Note: Listwise deletion of missing data within scales.

[a]The higher the score, the more satisfied the respondent.

Source: Stevens, Kiger, and Riley (2002)   [Research Navigator: 8768458]

of work on family cohesion. Even without knowing the exact wording of the items or how they were measured, this table provides important descriptive information about the scores on the different measures and whether these items are variable enough for further data analysis.

Identifying the Variables.   The table labels the dependent and independent variables. According to the complete article, "family cohesion" is measured with a nine-item scale with high scores reflecting more family cohesiveness. The scale scores represent an interval/ratio measure. "Emotion-work satisfaction" is a six-item scale and focuses on the emotional dimensions of the household work, especially with children; "household-task satisfaction" is one item asking respondents to indicate how satisfied they are with the amount of household tasks they share with their partners at home; "work-to-family spillover" is a six-item scale with higher scores indicating a high spillover negative effect of work on the family; "job satisfaction" uses a six-item scale; satisfaction with "family-friendly benefits" is a one-item scale with a score of seven indicating extreme satisfaction with the benefits supplied by work (child care, help with care of elder dependents, etc.); and "job flexibility" is measured with an eight-item scale.

All the dependent variables are interval/ratio measures. The article does not provide sample items for the scales, which can be obtained directly from the authors.

Interpreting the Table.   One way of interpreting Table 1.4 is to first see if each of the measures has enough variability for further data analysis. The standard deviation (SD) is one indicator of the spread of the scores around the mean (M) for the number (N) of people responding to that scale. If the standard deviation were zero for any of the variables, there would be no variability and those items could not be used. "Listwise deletion" in the footnote tells us that if a respondent (a case) did not answer an item that makes up a multiple item scale, then the entire case is deleted from the calculations.

Another way of reading the table is to compare men with women and get a sense if the sex of the person surveyed makes a difference in the scores. Only the average number of hours worked per week seems to differ, with women working fewer hours than men on average.

Making Conclusions and Explaining the Results.   The descriptive statistics for each of the scales suggest that there is some variability for both the men and the women in the study. These variables are suitable for further data analysis in the study. With the exception of number of hours worked per week, both men and women appear to report similar levels of satisfaction, perceptions of spillover impact of work on family, and family cohesiveness. How these independent variables explain the variation in family cohesiveness, the dependent variable, is discussed in the full article.

■ ■ ■ ■ ■

BOX 1.3

NOW IT'S YOUR TURN

A study was conducted to determine the personality traits of 72 college students who tend to hold paranormal beliefs. As is often customary, the journal article first reports some descriptive statistics about the sample. Here are data for those students who scored high and those students who scored low on a paranormal belief scale:

Descriptive Statistics for High and Low Paranormal Believers on the General Questionnaire (N = 72)

	LOW BELIEVERS		HIGH BELIEVERS	
Gender	Females	20	Females	23
	Males	16	Males	13
Self-Reported GPA (Median)	3.00		2.90	
Are you a religious person? (Median)	1.00 (Yes)		2.00 (Somewhat)	
How often do you attend church services within a month time period? (Median)	2–3 times/month		Once a month	
Do you believe in paranormal phenomena? (Yes)	33.3%		94.4%	
Do you have friends with similar paranormal beliefs? (Yes)	27.8%		100%	
Do you read materials/watch TV programs with paranormal themes? (Yes)	41.7%		66.7%	
How many hours per week do you spend reading materials or watching programs with paranormal themes? (15 hours or greater)	50%		72.2%	
Did you ever have an imaginary friend while growing up?	19.4%		41.7%	

Source: Auton, Pope, and Seeger (2005)   [Research Navigator: *11763486*]

QUESTIONS TO ANSWER:

1. What are the variables and their values? What are the levels of measurement for each of the variables?
2. What do the medians tell us? For example, what is a median of 2.90 for the high believers?
3. Describe in words what the table is showing us.
4. Can you conclude there is or isn't a difference in the characteristics of high and low believers?

SPSS OUTPUT

There are many ways to display data about a variable in SPSS. Graphs, frequency tables, and descriptive statistics are all important tools for understanding the distribution of a variable in a study.

Frequency Table

One of the first steps in data analysis is to see if there is a large enough range of responses for an item. Consider the frequency distribution in Table 1.5 for a question from the General Social Survey (GSS) about the number of children respondents have.

Identifying the Variables. *Number of children* is a discrete interval/ratio measure, although the last value "eight or more" technically does not allow us to get an exact number of children per family when there are more than seven. However, so few people (21 out of 1500) have that many children, it is not likely to distort any statistics or analyses that assume interval/ratio measures.

Interpreting the Table. The numbers in the left column are the valid answers (the values) to the question (the variable). This column also indicates

TABLE 1.5   Number of Children

		FREQUENCY	PERCENT	VALID PERCENT	CUMULATIVE PERCENT
Valid	0	414	27.6	27.7	27.7
	1	242	16.1	16.2	43.9
	2	398	26.5	26.6	70.5
	3	226	15.1	15.1	85.6
	4	115	7.7	7.7	93.3
	5	58	3.9	3.9	97.2
	6	14	.9	.9	98.1
	7	7	.5	.5	98.6
	Eight or More	21	1.4	1.4	100.0
	Total	1495	99.7	100.0	
Missing	NA	5	.3		
Total		1500	100.0		

Source: General Social Survey (GSS), 1993

the line that contains the total number of people who responded and the number of people who did not answer the question (the missing, here also labeled "NA" for "no answer" or "not applicable"), and then a grand total. The second column reports the actual raw numbers or frequency of occurrence for each value of the question, along with the total who responded, the number who left it blank, and the overall total number of respondents.

This second column of information (labeled "Frequency") tells us that 1500 people (the bottom line "Total") participated in the survey, although five ("Missing") did not respond to this particular question. Of the 1495 ("Total") who did answer the survey question, 414 have zero children, 242 have one child, and so on. The third column ("Percent") calculates the percentage each response represents out of the bottom line total, that is, out of 1500 possible respondents. For example, five people did not answer this question, so 5 divided by 1500 equals .003, or .3%. Out of 1500 possible respondents, 398 have two children, or 398/1500 = .265, or 26.5%.

Sometimes this information is important to have, but usually you want the percentage of people who actually answered the question. If a very large number of people do not answer a question, the percentages calculated in the "Percent" column could be exaggerated. As a result, SPSS also calculates the "Valid Percent" which is based only on the number of responses actually given. For example, 398 people said they have two children, but 398 divided by 1495 equals .266, or 26.6%. Note that in such cases where only a few people did not answer the question, the valid percent is very close to the percent. It all depends on your goal: Sometimes it's important to calculate a percentage based on the actual number of completed questions ("Valid Percent") and other times you want to know the percentage based on the number of people in the sample, including those who did not answer the question. This is usually the case when "No Answer" is considered to be an answer in itself. For example, a question on race/ethnicity might want to indicate the percentage of people who refuse to answer the question.

The final column, labeled "Cumulative Percent," is based on a running total of the Valid Percent. The valid percent for those with no children is 27.7% and for one child is 16.2%. The first number in the Cumulative percent column begins with the valid percent for the first value of 0. The second number is the accumulation of 27.7 plus the 16.2 for those who have one child, for a running total of 43.9. Now add in the percentage with two children (26.6) and you have a cumulative total of 70.5% (27.7 + 16.2 + 26.6 = 70.5). In words, you could say that 70.5% of the respondents who answered the question have two or fewer children. Notice that the last number in the Cumulative Percent column is 100% since all the valid percentages have been added together and should be similar to the total percent at the bottom line of the Valid Percent column. The Cumulative Percent does not use the Percent numbers; it is based only on those who answered the question, not the number of people who participated in the survey.

Cumulative percentages can only be used with data that are in order, such as ordinal and interval/ratio measures. It would not make sense to use this column of numbers for nominal data in which no order exists. Imagine a list of values for a question about "What kind of car do you drive?" that includes Toyota, Honda, Ford, Chevrolet, and so on. How could you say that 25% own a Honda or less? That would imply an order that is not there in nominal data.

Making Conclusions and Explaining the Results.   There appears to be enough variation in the answers to this question to warrant further use in more elaborate data analyses. Although most respondents have two or fewer children, the percentage of people with no children is almost similar to the percentage with two children, so you would have enough respondents, for example, to compare childless people with parents.

If we had information taken from a survey done in the 1920s or the 1960s, for example, we could compare whether the number of children people have today is smaller than in the past. We might see then that small family sizes are more typical in contemporary American society.

Bar Graph

Figure 1.4 illustrates the same results visually with a bar graph.

Identifying the Variables.   Although the variable "number of children" is an interval/ratio measure, it is also an example of discrete data. If this were

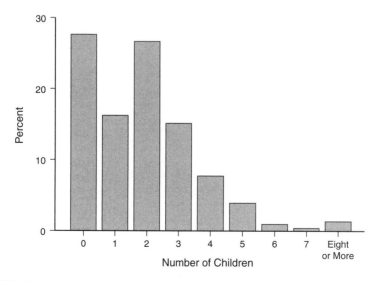

FIGURE 1.4

a continuous interval/ratio measure, a histogram would make a better choice because continuity between categories is indicated by the bars touching. Since it is not possible to have 2.3 or 1.8 children, for example, a bar graph portrays the discrete nature of this interval/ratio measure more accurately.

Interpreting the Graph.   Visually, it is evident that the most frequently occurring values are for the number of people with zero and two children, since they are the highest bars. Although the graph does not report the exact number, we can use this graph as a quick guide to viewing the distribution of responses to this variable. We can see that most people do not have large numbers of children and that the typical number of children is one, two, or three. Quite a few have no children, since this question was also answered by unmarried respondents.

Making Conclusions and Explaining the Results.   Again, we can conclude that contemporary American families tend to have small numbers of children. Why this is so, is not explained in this chart. These are descriptive data and are not set up to uncover explanations or predictions.

Descriptive Statistics

Another method for describing a variable and its responses is using statistical measures. Let's say you are interested in learning more about when and why people marry at different ages. Before you can do further data analysis, you must be sure the item in the survey is a variable in your sample. Table 1.6 gives the statistics that came attached to a frequency table showing the ages of first marriages among respondents to the GSS.

Identifying the Variables.   First it's important to know how a variable is measured before analyzing the statistics. Sometimes researchers provide an ordinal measure for age [such as (1) Under 20, (2) 20–30, (3) 31–40, (4) over 40] which would not be appropriate for calculating means and standard deviations. However, age is an interval/ratio measure in this survey and suitable for percentiles, means, and standard deviations.

Interpreting the Table.   There were 1202 people reporting the age they first married and 298 who did not. These are either people who never married or those who did but refused or forgot to answer the question. Of those who answered the question, the mathematical average age (the mean) was 22.79, or approximately, 23 years of age.

According to the median, half the respondents (that is, 601) got married before 22 years of age, and the other half got married over the age of 22. The most common age of first marriage (the mode) was 21. A frequency table would have to be consulted to get the exact percentage of the sample

TABLE 1.6   **Statistics**

AGE WHEN FIRST MARRIED		
N	Valid	1202
	Missing	298
Mean		22.79
Median		22.00
Mode		21
Std. Deviation		5.033
Range		45
Minimum		13
Maximum		58
Percentiles	25	19.00
	50	22.00
	75	25.00

Source: GSS 1993

that got married at 21. In this case, it was 11% according to the frequency table not shown here. Remember, you cannot say that the majority got married at 21, only that 21 was the most common age. After all, 89% did not get married at 21.

If the mean, median, and mode were the same, the distribution would be a normal curve, but here the mean is slightly higher than the median and mode, so it suggests that there are a few extremely high ages of first marriage. The complete frequency table shows at least one respondent who married for the first time at 13 and one at 58! This range of 45 years (58 − 13 = 45) combined with a standard deviation of only 5 years indicates that—although there are some extreme answers—most respondents are probably clustered within plus or minus 5 years of 23.

The percentiles tell us more about the distribution. Here the percentiles are given for every quarter of the distribution; these are called the *quartiles.* Notice that the 50th percentile is the same as the median, as it should be. The percentiles show that 25% of the sample married at 19 or younger, 75% married at 25 or younger, or conversely, that 25% of the sample got married for the first time at or after the age of 25. These *quartiles* could be used to calculate an interquartile range (for example, the 75th–25th range would be 25 − 22 = 3 years).

Making Conclusions and Explaining the Results.   This questionnaire item appears to be a variable with some dispersion of ages suitable for further data analysis. Even though you may not know many people who marry as young as 23, remember these numbers are aggregated data. That is, it combines all 1202 people; for a better understanding of age of first marriage, disaggregating the data by gender (do men or women marry younger?), region of the country, religious background, educational level, and other important variables would tell us much more than the overall descriptive statistics do. But in order to do these analyses, it's important to first establish that you have variables; for example, if 90% of the sample was from the Midwest, then where respondents live would not be a useful variable to understand regional differences in marriage age.

■ ■ ■ ■ ■ ▨▨

BOX 1.4

NOW IT'S YOUR TURN

Respondents to the GSS were asked to indicate approximately how many hours per day they typically watch television.

Hours per Day Watching TV

		FREQUENCY	PERCENT	VALID PERCENT	CUMULATIVE PERCENT
Valid	0	56	3.7	3.8	3.8
	1	311	20.7	20.9	24.6
	2	422	28.1	28.3	53.0
	3	282	18.8	18.9	71.9
	4	183	12.2	12.3	84.2
	5	95	6.3	6.4	90.6
	6	67	4.5	4.5	95.1
	7	10	.7	.7	95.8
	8	32	2.1	2.1	97.9
	9	2	.1	.1	98.1
	10	15	1.0	1.0	99.1
	12	8	.5	.5	99.6
	16	2	.1	.1	99.7
	20	2	.1	.1	99.9
	22	1	.1	.1	99.9
	24	1	.1	.1	100.0
	Total	1489	99.3	100.0	
Missing	NA	11	.7		
Total		1500	100.0		

(continued)

■ ■ ■ ■

BOX 1.4 CONTINUED

Statistics

HOURS PER DAY WATCHING TV		
N	Valid	1489
	Missing	11
Mean		2.90
Median		2.00
Mode		2
Std. Deviation		2.238
Range		24
Percentiles	25	2.00
	50	2.00
	75	4.00

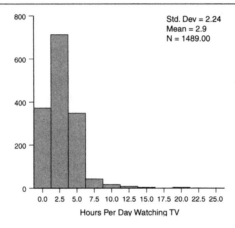

Std. Dev = 2.24
Mean = 2.9
N = 1489.00

Hours Per Day Watching TV

QUESTIONS TO ANSWER:

1. What is the variable and level of measurement?
2. Which of the statistics are relevant to use?
3. What do the percent, valid percent, and cumulative percent tell us? How many people answered the question? How many people were in the sample?
4. Describe in words what the frequency table is presenting. For example, what does the 6.4 in the valid percent column tell us? To get you started: 6.4% of . . .
5. Interpret the mean, median, mode, range, standard deviation, and percentiles.
6. Why is a histogram suitable to use here? Interpret the graph.
7. Put into everyday words what the survey tells us about Americans' television viewing.
8. What could be plausible explanations for the results? Are there any theories or previous research that can guide you in interpreting the findings?

SUMMING UP DESCRIPTIVE STATISTICS, TABLES, AND GRAPHS

As a first step in data analysis, it's important to establish how many items in a survey are actual variables useful for more complex statistical procedures. In addition, describing the characteristics of respondents, highlighting some key findings, and discussing any patterns depend on the use of visual charts or graphs, frequency tables, and statistical measures of central tendency and dispersion.

When reading public opinion poll results or interpreting the pie charts or bar graphs typical of most figures in the popular media, it's essential to understand the way the variables are measured and how the questions were asked. Variations in wording can lead to many different results and the use of an incorrect statistic or graph can easily create false interpretations, as Darrel Huff (1954) demonstrated in his classic book *How to Lie with Statistics*.

Although presenting univariate information is common, more typical of academic research, newspaper reports, and surveys is the display of bivariate data. Rarely do we want to just know information about each variable. More likely, we want to know the relationship between two variables, or among three or more, in helping us to explain the results. Bivariate and multivariate analyses are central to understanding complex behavior and opinions. With this in mind, the next chapter turns to bivariate data and the interpretation of tables in which two variables are presented in relationship to one another.

CHAPTER 2

UNDERSTANDING
TABLES

One of the central goals of research is to describe, explain, or predict relationships between two or more variables. Although a good first step is to describe the distribution of each variable in a study, as illustrated in the previous chapter, analyzing the relationship of two or more variables is essential. For example, finding out the distribution of political party preferences and the number of men and women among the respondents in a public opinion poll of voting behavior is important, but even more relevant is an analysis of which sex was more or less likely to support particular political candidates.

One way of uncovering these bivariate relationships requires comparing two variables simultaneously and constructing a single table showing the distributions of the two variables. These are called *cross-tabulations* or *contingency tables*. The resulting table is one of the most used methods to display data in popular publications, scholarly journals, and professional reports. This chapter explains how to read tables, make sense of the data, and put the information presented into clear, everyday language.

DEFINITIONS

■ **Cross-tabulations** or **Contingency Tables** are constructed of frequency distributions for two variables (bivariate) presented simultaneously. We hypothesize that the distribution of values of one variable (the dependent or outcome variable) is *contingent* or dependent on the distribution of values of the other variable (the independent, predictor, or causal variable). These tables are sometimes simply called *crosstabs.*

■ **Rows, Columns, and Cells** are key to understanding crosstabulations. The format of a table is similar to any spreadsheet, like the ones used in Excel or SPSS. It's simple to remember the format if you visualize a seating chart in a theater: as you walk down the aisle to your seat you are looking for a *row* and you go *across* to that seat. If you look back and forward you can see everyone who is seated in your *column*. In other words, your row number or letter represents the row which goes across from left to right, and your seat number is the column which goes from top to bottom (or in a theater, from back to front). So if you have a ticket for M24, you are in the M row in seat 24 in front of the person in N24 and in back of seat L24. Rows go across left to right (horizontal), and columns, like those that hold up a building, go up and down (vertical). A table is often described in terms of its rows and columns, so a table with three rows and four columns would be a 3 by 4 table (sometimes depicted as 3x4). The point where a row and column meet in a table is referred to as a *cell*. For example, you might refer to a number in a table by locating the cell in row 3, column 2.

ASSUMPTIONS

- Cross-tabulations are ideally suited to variables measured using nominal or ordinal level discrete categories. It is very difficult to read tables with numerous rows and columns, thus making crosstabs not the best way to depict continuous interval/ratio level measurements that have many values or categories.
- For easier interpretation, many researchers build the tables with the independent variable's categories in the columns and the dependent variable's values in the rows. However, based on the size of the table, it is sometimes preferable to present the independent variable in the rows and the dependent variable in the columns.
- Tables are best read when percentages are also given along with the frequencies. Each category or value of the independent variable must add up to 100% in order to compare the influence of the different categories of the independent variable on the dependent variable outcomes. This is especially important if there is a different total number of responses in each of the variable's categories. When the columns contain the independent variable categories, each column's category must add up to 100%. If rows are used for the independent variable, each row category must then total 100%.

DATA FROM POPULAR PUBLICATIONS

Let's begin by illustrating typical crosstabs as they appear in daily newspapers when information is presented from public opinion polls.

TABLE 2.1   **View of Constitutional Amendment Depends on the Context**

	ASKED AFTER GAY MARRIAGE %	ASKED BEFORE GAY MARRIAGE %
Favor amendment	48	54
Oppose amendment	47	41
Don't know	5	5
	100	100

(*Source:*) Los Angeles *Times* (June 2004) "Do you favor or oppose an amendment to the U.S. Constitution that legally defines marriage as a union between a man and a woman only, and would prevent states from legally recognizing same-sex marriages?" Question rotated with baseline measure of support or opposition to gay marriage.

Simple Bivariate Table

Table 2.1 shows the results from a June 2004 *Los Angeles Times* poll on support of or opposition to "an amendment to the U.S. Constitution that legally defines marriage as a union between a man and a woman only, and would prevent states from legally recognizing same-sex marriages." This question was posed in some situations after respondents were first asked their opinion about gay marriages. For others, they received this question before they were asked about gay marriages. These data therefore show not only opinions about the amendment, but illustrate the importance of knowing the order in which questions are asked.

Identifying the Variables.   The first step is to identify what the variables are in the cross-tabulation and why this is an appropriate format to use with these variables. Typically the labels for the categories of each variable are placed outside the table or can be listed in the first row and column of the table. In this example, the top row contains the two categories (or values) of the variable "order of question": "Asked after gay marriage" question and "Asked before gay marriage" question. This is a nominal level dichotomy (two values).

The rows contain three values (favor, oppose, don't know) of the main variable about favoring or opposing the Constitutional amendment. This is a nominal level measure. Both variables are thus suitable for a crosstab and the use of percentages.

As a rule of thumb, the categories of the independent variable should add up to 100%. Therefore, this table tells us that the context of asking the question before or after the gay marriage question is the independent variable.

Interpreting the Table.   Notice that each column adds up to 100. Therefore, these numbers are percentages and not just raw frequency counts, unless there were exactly 100 people who heard the question before and 100 people who heard the question about the Constitutional amendment after one on their position on gay marriage. This would make the raw numbers the same as the percentage, but here the raw numbers (frequency counts) are not supplied. Given the rule that each value of the independent variable must add up to 100%, the table also tells us that question order is the independent variable. Whether respondents support or oppose the amendment depends on the order in which they hear the questions, so opinion about the amendment is the dependent or outcome variable. The table's label also tells us that the view of the Constitutional amendment "depends on the context," making respondents' opinions the dependent variable. Attitudes depend on the context.

In other words, people's responses are contingent on order of the questions. Another way is to say that question order predicts respondents' attitudes about the Constitutional amendment. Since these are findings about a large group of people, you cannot make conclusions about any one person in the sample or generalize to all Americans, unless you are assured this sample was randomly selected from the population.

The table tells us that 48% of people who were asked about the Constitutional amendment after their opinion about gay marriage favor the amendment compared with 54% of those who were asked about the amendment first. It looks as if hearing the amendment question first resulted in greater support of the amendment than for those who heard it second after the question about gay marriage. The table does *not* state that 48% of those who favor the amendment heard about the gay marriage question first and that 54% of those who favor the amendment heard the gay marriage second. This is a key point and often confusing to many people. Take another example: just because 65% of sociology students on campus are women, it does not mean that 65% of women are sociology majors. Think about the different meanings here when reading a contingency table.

Remember, the percentages are based on the number of people within each independent variable category. It is very important to read tables by comparing *across* the categories of the independent variable. This is why each value or category must add up to 100% so comparisons can be made across the values.

Making Conclusions and Explaining the Results.   A reasonable conclusion is that order of questions makes a difference in public opinion polls. Asking about gay marriage first results in a virtual tie in opinion about favoring or opposing the Constitutional amendment and contrasts with those who did not hear the gay marriage question first. They were more likely to favor the Constitutional amendment. Whether these numbers are statistically significant findings—that is, likely to have occurred this way by chance fewer than 5 times out of 100 (p < .05)—is not typically presented in popular mass media publications. Scholarly research, however, requires that significance levels of statistical analyses be presented and that visual conclusions not be made simply by reading the table as we've done here. Chapter Three explains how to interpret the statistics typically used with cross-tabulations.

It is important also to see what the sampling error for the sample in a poll is before making final conclusions. The typical *Los Angeles Times* poll has a sampling error of plus or minus 4%. This tells us that, with the number of respondents surveyed, generalizing to the entire national population must take into account the possibility of some error. That is, if the result for a "Yes" answer is 70% of all respondents then the true percentage in the entire U.S. population is somewhere between 66% and 74% (that is, 70 − 4 = 66 and 70 + 4 = 74). It is not exactly 70%. In the table presented here, there is a 6% difference (48% versus 54%) between the two groups so it might be reasonable to conclude (even though we cannot statistically conclude) that the order of the question might make some difference in whether people are in favor of this Constitutional amendment.

Why there are differences cannot be determined from this table. Perhaps those who heard the amendment question first also used it to express their opposition to gay marriage, whereas those who had the opportunity to express themselves first about gay marriage now were able to focus solely on the appropriateness of a Constitutional amendment. A literature review of studies that focus on questionnaire construction also might provide some evidence of the impact of question order.

Multiple Variables Crosstabs

Another typical way of presenting data is Table 2.2 from a June 2004 poll of 3000 adults in the United States, conducted by the *Pew Research Center for the People and the Press* that looked at TV and radio news popularity by political affiliation. This table is somewhat different from the earlier ones in that each column does not add up to 100%. Rather, each cell reports only the "Regularly" responses. Also each row represents a different variable; these are not 13 categories or values of a single variable because they are not mutually exclusive categories. People did not have to choose only one source for news. Each row in this table is a summary of a larger table of data; these numbers represent the results from 13 different crosstabs.

Identifying the Variables. The independent variable is political party affiliation with the nominal category values of Republican, Democrat, and Independent represented. The dependent variables are a set of 13 television and radio news shows and networks, such as CNN and the "Daily Show."

TABLE 2.2   **Partisans Using Different Sources**

PERCENT WHO REGULARLY WATCH...	TOTAL %	REP %	DEM %	IND %
Fox News Channel	25	**35**	21	22
CNN	22	19	**28**	22
MSNBC	11	10	12	12
CNBC	10	9	12	9
NBC Nightly News	17	15	18	19
CBS Evening News	16	13	**19**	17
ABC World News	16	15	20	12
NPR	16	13	**19**	17
NewsHour	5	**4**	5	5
O'Reilly Factor	8	**16**	3	6
Rush Limbaugh	6	**14**	2	4
Larry King	5	5	6	3
Daily Show	3	3	3	3

Source: Pew Research Center for the People and the Press (June 2004)

Respondents were asked to indicate whether they watched or listened to each of these shows regularly, sometimes, hardly ever, or never. This is an ordinal measure and the table reports only the percentages of respondents who selected "regularly" for each of the news shows. The hypothesis is that viewing or listening to different news shows depends on respondents' political affiliations.

Essentially what is presented are the results of 13 different crosstabs in which political party is the independent variable and frequency of viewing a news show is the dependent variable. Only the "regularly" results are presented on each line. Taking the first row, for example, Fox News Channel, 25% of the entire sample responded that they regularly watched that channel; therefore, 75% watched it sometimes, hardly ever, and never. These last data are not presented in the table so we cannot actually tell how many watched Fox "sometimes" or "never." The original table probably looked something like Table 2.3 (although with actual percentages for the sometimes, hardly ever, and never categories):

Interpreting the Table.   The Pew Research Center report highlights some patterns: Republicans tend to watch Fox News Channel regularly more than other stations or shows, along with Bill O'Reilly and Rush Limbaugh, compared to Democrats, who favor CNN, CBS, and NPR (National Public Radio).

TABLE 2.3

FOX NEWS CHANNEL	TOTAL	REPUBLICAN	DEMOCRAT	INDEPENDENT
Regularly	25%	35%	21%	22%
Sometimes	xx	xx	xx	xx
Hardly Ever	xx	xx	xx	xx
Never	xx	xx	xx	xx
Total	100%	100%	100%	100%

In words, you would say that 35% of Republicans watch Fox regularly compared to 21% of Democrats and 22% of Independents. Note that this does not say that 35% of Fox viewers are Republican. These data cannot be determined from this table.

The Total column tells us that, regardless of political party loyalties, the overall sample of 3000 respondents favor Fox News, CNN, NBC, CBS, ABC, and NPR for their daily news. In many statistical programs and published tables, the Total column often appears last rather than first as in this report. One way of interpreting tables is to look at the Total figures and ask whether each group is more, less, or the same as the overall total. For example, 5% of the respondents regularly watch Larry King, but so do about the same percentage of Republicans (5%), Democrats (6%), and Independents (3%). In other words, political party affiliation does not help us in predicting who will watch Larry King's news show. However, compare the overall total of respondents who watch CNN (22%) to the 28% of Democrats who watch CNN and the 19% of Republicans. Clearly, Democrats are higher than the norm (22%) and Republicans have lower viewing rates than the overall figures of CNN. Using the Total column is helpful in making these interpretations.

Making Conclusions and Explaining the Results.   A pattern appears to be emerging with the conservative news station—Fox—and the conservative hosts, namely O'Reilly and Limbaugh, who are listened to more regularly by Republicans than by Democrats or Independents. Democrats tend to favor CNN and NPR. In other words, there seems to be a political party relationship to choice of news shows.

The reasons for the political party differences in the selection of news shows are not presented in this table. Perhaps a content analysis of the shows that explores the language, biases, and images displayed on each network would indicate some of the reasons. These findings are a good example of how one set of data can generate new research questions and methodologies for further investigation.

■ ■ ■ ■ ■

BOX 2.1

NOW IT'S YOUR TURN

In 2003, 1200 adults were asked in a nationwide survey by the *Pew Research Center for the People and the Press:* "In order to overcome past discrimination, do you favor or oppose affirmative action programs designed to help blacks, women and other minorities get better jobs and education?" They also responded to another question: "All in all, do you think affirmative action programs designed to increase the number of black and minority students on college campuses are a good thing or a bad thing?" Here are two crosstabs reporting the results comparing white men and women.

Gender Gap on Affirmative Action

PROGRAMS THAT ...

... help blacks, women and other minorities get jobs & education	*White Women %*	*White Man %*
Favor	66	48
Oppose	26	41
Don't know	8	11
	100	100

... raise # of minority college students		
Good thing	60	48
Bad thing	28	43
Don't know	12	9
	100	100

QUESTIONS TO ANSWER:

1. Which are the independent and dependent variables and what are their levels of measurement (nominal, ordinal, interval/ratio)?
2. What hypothesis is being tested?
3. Why is a crosstab suitable here?
4. What do the percentages indicate? Describe in words what the table is showing us. For example, what does the 26 in the second row say? To get you started: 26% of ...
5. Make a conclusion about the Pew Poll results using everyday language.
6. Can you comfortably conclude that there is or is not a "gender gap" here? What else would help you make a conclusion?
7. What could be plausible explanations for the results? Are there any theories or previous research that can guide you in interpreting the findings?

SCHOLARLY ARTICLE

Tables showing the relationship between two or more variables appear often in academic articles, usually accompanied by statistics showing if the depicted relationship is statistically significant. Chapter Three illustrates the statistics, so let's first demonstrate how tables are used in articles and learn how to interpret them.

Simple Bivariate Table

Stein (1998) reports on a study of voting behavior in Texas during a gubernatorial election. He was interested in seeing if there was a difference in several demographic characteristics between those who voted on Election Day and those who voted early. In Texas, people can choose to vote in person at designated sites during the three weeks leading up to Election Day. Nearly 30% voted early in Texas. Table 2.4 presents some results:

TABLE 2.4   Selected Characteristics of Early and Election-Day Voters (Percent by Column)

VARIABLE	ELECTION DAY (N = 1,362)	EARLY (N = 1,531)
PARTY IDENTIFICATION		
Strong Republican	24.8	26.9
Republican	6.9	4.6
Weak Republican	2.5	1.7
Independent	26.5	27
Weak Democrat	2.4	1.5
Democrat	8.0	6.2
Strong Democrat	29	32
GENDER		
Male	47.6	52.1
Female	52.4	47.9
EDUCATION		
Less than high school	7.1	7.5
High school graduate	20	22.3
Some college	33.1	30
College graduate	24.3	22.2
Postgraduate study	15.5	18

Source: Stein (1998)

Identifying the Variables.   This table is labeled with the phrase "percent by column." Because we know that tables are constructed with the categories of the variable to be compared each adding up to 100%, this statement tells us (without having to add the numbers up ourselves) that the comparison is between those who vote early and those who vote on Election Day. One could say that the variable is "Timing of Voting" which has two values or categories: "Election Day" or "Early."

There are three different demographic variables forming the rows— Party Identification, Gender, and Education—so three separate contingency tables or crosstabs actually make up this one table.

Relevant hypotheses might ask what characteristics predict who will vote early. Does educational level affect the time of voting? Does voting early depend on party affiliation, education, or gender? And could the time of voting in turn affect the outcomes of the election? In other words, time of voting could serve as either independent or dependent variables, based on what the research focus is. These are some of the questions the research addresses, but the first goal was simply to describe the characteristics of early voters versus Election Day voters.

This is a reminder that you must first be clear what the goals of the research and what your research questions are before designing tables. In this case, the objective is to compare across the two categories of timing of vote, so these then become the columns each adding up to 100% in order to make the comparison. This is one of those situations in which it is not particularly important to label which ones are the independent and dependent variables because we cannot say that voting early comes before, causes, or predicts educational level, gender, or party affiliation. Rather, the goal is simply descriptive comparisons between two voting periods; this goal then determines the direction of the percentages, in this case the columns comparing the categories representing the time of voting.

The variables in the tables are either dichotomies (two categories, such as Election Day or Early, and gender) or ordinal level discrete measures (the categories of party identification and education both have an order to them so they are more than nominal measures). All variables are therefore suitable for cross-tabulations.

Interpreting the Table.   The null hypothesis would be that the people who vote early are not different from the people who vote on Election Day. Let's look at the first crosstab with Party Identification. Note that the sample sizes (*N*) are fairly close: 1,362 people in the sample voted on Election Day and 1,531 voted early. Because there are not exactly the same numbers of people in each category of the variable, percentages are reported in order to make comparisons between the two categories. Of those voting on Election Day, 24.8% were strong Republicans compared with 26.9% of those voting early. Although this is a difference, it does not look to be very large. In fact, if you add up the percentages of all Republicans (Strong to Weak), you see that 34.2% of those voting on Election Day are Republicans compared with 33.2% of those voting early. These numbers are not likely to be statistically different.

Similarly, 39.4% of those voting on Election Day are Democrats compared with 39.7% of those voting early—virtually a tie. In other words, the political profiles of those voters who vote at two different times are essentially the same. Recall that the data do not tell us *the percentage of Democrats* who voted early or on Election Day. It is not the same as saying that 39.4% of registered Democrats voted on Election Day. We don't know this information from the table. Instead, these numbers are the percentage *of those voting* on Election Day who are Democrat compared to the percentage of those voting early who are Democrat. If you wanted to compare the voting behaviors of Democrats and Republicans, then you would need to calculate the percentages differently in order to compare these two categories. Party Identification might make up the columns and timing of the vote categories would make up the rows. Then you can say that a certain percentage of Democrats voted early compared with a certain percentage of Republicans.

There do appear to be somewhat larger differences in gender between those who voted early and those who voted on Election Day. While 47.9% of those who voted early are female, 52.4% of those who voted on Election Day are female. These differences may be statistically significant. Remember, the data do *not* tell us what percentage of women voted early compared with voting on Election Day.

Comparing percentages between those who voted early with those who voted on Election Day, the results for Education appear not to be very different: 15.5% of those who voted on Election Day completed some graduate school work compared with 18% of those who voted early. Again, the table does *not* say that 18% of those with graduate school work voted early. We cannot compare differences among the five levels of education in terms of the timing of their voting. To compare across the categories of education (and make it the independent variable), each category must be recalculated to add up to 100%.

Making Conclusions and Explaining the Results. From these data, we can conclude that a larger percentage of men vote early compared with the percentage who vote on Election Day. Otherwise, there are no differences in actual party affiliation and educational levels between the two subgroups. Early voters yield about the same percentage of Democrats and Republicans turning out as those who vote on Election Day. The published article goes into much more detail with additional variables and more sophisticated statistical analysis. It uses these demographic variables along with some measures of political partisanship to analyze actual voting choices in the election.

Why there would be gender differences and not political party or educational ones may have several possible explanations. The data presented here don't help us in explaining the results, so speculation based on hunches or previous research and theory might guide us in making sense of these findings. People who are more interested in politics and partisan in their views tend to vote early more than those who are not as interested or as partisan. Could men in Texas be more politically involved and more committed to particular views than women? Another possibility may be job-related, with the convenience of voting early or with absentee ballots following gender differences in work. Reading other studies or conducting further research might explain the differences between men and women in their voting patterns.

The point to remember is that once you get one set of results, your task has just begun. Descriptive findings like these data typically lead to another set of more complex and sophisticated research questions.

Multivariate Crosstabs

Comparing two variables is often a good start, but usually there is a need to include additional variables in the analysis. Table 2.5 compares 73 boys' and girls' (fourth and fifth graders) perceptions of the source and stability of conflicts with friends. Students were asked "Why do you think fights with friends happen at all?" and their responses were coded with two variables: attributed source of the conflict and judgment about the stability or impermanence of the conflict.

Identifying the Variables.   Three variables are present: sex of respondent (boys or girls), a nominal dichotomy; stability or impermanence of the con-

TABLE 2.5   **Attribution Regarding Stability of Causes of Conflicts with Friends**

	STABLES (N = 25)		IMPERMANENT (N = 48)		TOTAL (N = 73)
	Girls (n = 16)	Boys (n = 9)	Girls (n = 23)	Boys (n = 25)	
Human or relationship characteristic	16 (100.0)	8 (88.9)	6 (26.1)	3 (12.0)	33 (45.2)
International condition	0 (0.0)	1 (11.1)	11 (47.8)	14 (56.0)	26 (35.6)
Person characteristics	0 (0.0)	0 (0.0)	6 (26.1)	7 (28.0)	13 (17.8)
Extraneous characteristics	0 (0.0)	0 (0.0)	0 (0.0)	1 (4.0)	1 (1.4)

Note: Numbers in parentheses indicate column percentages.

Source: Joshi and Ferris, 2002   [Research Navigator: 8768455]

flict, also a nominal dichotomy; and the attributed cause, a nominal variable: human or relationship characteristic (cause is due to the nature of friendships or people, such as "people are different"), interactional condition (conflicting goals that come up in a friendship), person characteristics (actions or attributes of the other or self, such as "she was in a bad mood"), extraneous characteristics (things external to the relationship). In this case the attributed cause is the dependent variable, sex is the independent variable, and the stability/impermanence of the conflict is the third variable, often called a control variable.

Nominal variables are ideally suited to cross-tabulations and percentage distributions.

Interpreting the Table.   With three variables, the table can be read in several ways. Begin by looking at the overall summary of the findings by reading the Total results in the last (marginal) column. Almost half of the children (45.2%) attribute the cause of conflicts with friends to human or relationship characteristics, that is, to the nature of people and friendships. Over one-third (35.6%) see the source as due to interactional conditions that arise in the course of a friendship.

Now compare these overall numbers to the findings between boys and girls within each category of the control variable. We can see that for those children who view their conflicts with friends as stable, there is very little gender difference. Both boys and girls attribute the stable conflicts to the nature of friendships and humans (100% versus 88.9%), but much more so than the overall results (45.2%).

However, for those conflicts they view as temporary or impermanent, boys seem to attribute their causes more to interactional conditions than girls do (56% versus 47.8%). Furthermore, both boys and girls see impermanent conflicts much more likely attributable to person characteristics than the overall total percentages (26.1% and 28% versus total of 17.8%).

Making Conclusions and Explaining the Results.   Boys are slightly more likely to attribute the causes of conflicts, especially temporary ones, to interactions during a friendship compared to girls who tend to explain conflict as something due to the nature of friendships and being human. However, for both boys and girls, the sense of the conflict as ongoing or temporary yields different explanations: stable conflicts with friends are due to the nature of friendship or humans, while impermanent ones are attributed to the interaction or the individual persons involved.

Some developmental theories explain that as children grow older they tend to look more for situational explanations than for reasons that are inherent in people. Perhaps as children view the conflicts with friends as more temporary they begin to see how much of conflict depends on the situations. As always, further research into these ideas needs to be done.

■ ■ ■ ■ ■

BOX 2.2

NOW IT'S YOUR TURN

Looker and Thiessen (1999) interviewed 1700 Canadian 17-year olds about their images of women's work and men's work. Here are their responses concerning their willingness to consider an occupation associated with the other sex.

Attitude to taking a job associated with the other gender by the gender of youth respondent.

WOULD YOU CONSIDER AN OCCUPATION THAT IS MOSTLY MALE/ FEMALE NOW?

	Definitely	*Probably*	*Probably not*	*Definitely not*	*N*
Gender of respondent:					
Male	9%	42%	42%	7%	555
Female	32%	48%	18%	3%	633
Total	21%	45%	29%	5%	1,188

Source: Looker and Thiessen (1999)

QUESTIONS TO ANSWER:

1. Which are the independent and dependent variables and what are their levels of measurement?
2. What hypothesis is being tested?
3. Do the columns or rows add up to 100%? Why does this help in interpreting the data?
4. Describe in words what the table is showing us. For example, what is the 42 in row one, column three? Put it into words. To get you started: 42% of . . .
5. Make a conclusion about the results using everyday language.
6. Can you conclude that there is or is not a gender difference here? What else would help you make a conclusion?
7. What could be plausible explanations for the results? Are there any theories or previous research that can guide you in interpreting the findings?

SPSS OUTPUT

When writing an article for publication in a newspaper or scholarly journal, authors don't simply take the output from a statistical program and plop it into the article as is. What you see may not look the way it comes out of the computer program. For this reason, SPSS output is included here for your interpretation.

Bivariate Tables

Table 2.6 shows some crosstabulation data using the General Social Survey (GSS) to test the relationship between race and attitudes toward rap music. This is a national random sample of people throughout the United States 18 years of age and older.

Identifying the Variables.   SPSS prints the variable labels and value labels clearly in the crosstabulation. The columns represent "Race" broken down into three categories or values: white, black, and other. There were too few Latinos and Asians who completed the survey to include them in separate categories so they are combined with other smaller groups in "Other." The rows represent attitudes toward "Rap Music" and include "Like It," "Mixed Feelings," and "Dislike It."

The "Total" column simply refers to all respondents aggregated, that is, the summation of everyone's responses about each category of rap music opinion regardless of race. The responses are not disaggregated by (broken down into subgroups of) race; the total numbers are the simple univariate descriptive results from the 1431 respondents on this one questionnaire item (13% Like it, and so on). Some tables also show the totals for each column and place them in the last or bottom row (in this case, 1201 of the respondents are

TABLE 2.6   **Rap Music * Race of Respondent Crosstabulation**

| | | | Race of Respondent | | | |
			white	*black*	*other*	*Total*
Rap	Like it	Count	117	52	17	186
Music		% within Race of Respondent	9.7%	32.3%	24.6%	13.0%
	Mixed Feelings	Count	205	41	20	266
		% within Race of Respondent	17.1%	25.5%	29.0%	18.6%
	Dislike It	Count	879	68	32	979
		% within Race of Respondent	73.2%	42.2%	46.4%	68.4%
Total		Count	1201	161	69	1431
		% within Race of Respondent	100.0%	100.0%	100.0%	100.0%

white). The rows and columns containing the totals are called the *marginals* because they are not in the center of the table but on the edges or margins. These marginal rows and columns are not counted as part of the table size, so in this case, the table is 3×3, that is, three rows and three columns of data, not counting any rows or columns containing "total" numbers.

Because the columns add up to 100%, we can compare the respondents' attitudes toward rap (dependent variable) across the three categories or values of race (independent variable). In other words, we are asking whether taste in rap music depends on race. Do blacks or whites or other groups prefer rap more? Does knowing race predict attitudes toward music?

Because the goal is to describe differences in attitudes by race, and because race is a nominal measure and attitude toward rap is an ordinal measure, a crosstab or contingency table is a good choice for presenting the results.

Interpreting the Table.   By looking at the Total in the marginal column, we can first see that, overall, the majority (68.4%) of people dislike rap and the rest have mixed or positive opinions about the music. When we disaggregate race into the three categories, however, a different pattern emerges. Only whites have a majority (73.2%) who dislike rap music and 9.7% who like it. Compare 73.2% with the minority (42.2%) of black respondents and the Other (46.4%) group of people who dislike rap.

Again, look across the categories of the independent variable, each of which has been standardized by converting the raw numbers to percentages. Here is a good example why percentages are needed. If you just had the frequency counts, you might conclude that whites like rap more (117) than blacks (52) and others (17) do. But there are many more whites completing the survey, so any raw numbers must be converted to percentages in order to compare unequal subgroups. Therefore, 117 divided by 1201 whites in the sample (marginal total for the column labeled white) results in 9.7% of whites liking rap.

Also remember that these data show that 9.7% of whites like rap, not that 9.7% of those who like rap are white. If you want to find out the characteristics of those who like rap music, then you must compute row percentages and divide, for example, the 117 whites who like rap by the total number of people in the survey who like rap (186) to show that 63% of respondents in the sample who like rap music are white. By comparing this percentage to the population's distribution of whites, you can make conclusions whether fans of rap music are disproportionately or proportionately white.

Making Conclusions and Explaining the Results.   Putting the findings into everyday language, we can say the following: Although the majority of people do not like rap music, blacks report they like rap music more than whites do; in fact, almost three times as many say this (32.3% versus 9.7%). Those who are in the Other subgroup also like rap more than whites, but to a slightly lesser degree than blacks.

Why there are racial differences in attitudes toward rap cannot be determined by this table. Further analysis with other variables needs to be done in order to explain the outcomes. Perhaps age is a factor and if only people between the ages of 18 and 30 were analyzed, then the majority in all categories of race might like rap. Or maybe even in that age range, the majority of respondents dislikes it and differences by race continue to emerge. Knowledge of previous scholarly research on music tastes and race/ethnicity differences helps in developing theories to guide explanations of research findings.

Multivariate Tables

A more complicated type of analysis involves multiple independent variables and one dependent variable. For example, imagine we are interested in analyzing attendance at art museums in the past year. Age is a likely variable in explaining attendance, and so might be sex of the respondents. Table 2.7 on page 48 looks at both simultaneously with data from the GSS.

Identifying the Variables. Visiting an art museum is a nominal variable measured simply as a dichotomy (yes/no). Attendance is dependent on age, which is divided into ordinal categories, and on sex, also a nominal dichotomy. The hypothesis being tested is that age and sex explain museum attendance.

Interpreting the Table. What appears as one large cross-tabulation can be viewed as two separate tables, one each for the categories of the third variable, in this case, sex. Take the Male table first and read the crosstab between age and museum attendance. For example, 38.0% of 18–29 year old men visited an art museum or gallery in the past year. This number is compared across the age categories in order to see if there is an age difference among the men. It seems that 40 to 49 year old men visit the museum more often (46.1%) than men in other age categories; men 50 and over attend the least (31.2%). In each age category, the majority of men did not go to an art museum or gallery last year.

Now take a look at the women. Similarly, attendance was highest among the 40 to 49 year olds, and the lowest was among women 50 and older.

But what about sex of the respondents as an explanation instead of age? This variable can be evaluated by comparing men and women within age categories, that is, compare the 18 to 29 year old women with the 18 to 29 year old men. Here we see that 46.5% of 18-29 year old women visited an art museum last year compared with 38.0% of 18–29 year old men. In fact, in each age category, women appear to have slightly higher rates of attendance than

TABLE 2.7 Visited Art Museum or Gallery in Last Yr * Age Categories * Respondent's Sex Crosstabulation

Respondent's Sex			AGE CATEGORIES					
			18–29	30–39	40–49	50+	Total
Male	Visited Art Museum or Gallery in Last Yr	Yes	Count	46	66	65	68	245
			% within Age Categories	38.0%	41.8%	46.1%	31.2%	38.4%
		No	Count	75	92	76	150	393
			% within Age Categories	62.0%	58.2%	53.9%	68.8%	61.6%
	Total		Count	121	158	141	218	638
			% within Age Categories	100.0%	100.0%	100.0%	100.0%	100.0%
Female	Visited Art Museum or Gallery in Last Yr	Yes	Count	73	88	81	115	357
			% within Age Categories	46.5%	45.8%	49.1%	34.2%	42.0%
		No	Count	84	104	84	221	493
			% within Age Categories	53.5%	54.2%	50.9%	65.8%	58.0%
	Total		Count	157	192	165	336	850
			% within Age Categories	100.0%	100.0%	100.0%	100.0%	100.0%

men do. The difference is especially strong for the youngest category of respondents. The other differences do not seem as large: men and women in the other age groupings have more similar museum attendance patterns.

Making Conclusions and Explaining the Results.   Can we conclude there is an age or sex difference in attending museums? It appears that older people visit the least, so age is likely a relevant variable. And more women go to museums than men do, so sex is possibly an important variable as well, but perhaps not as strong as the age variable. The sex differences do not seem as large in all but the youngest group. Knowing just one variable helps us to explain museum attendance; knowing the interactive impact of both sex and age provides even more depth to this analysis.

Introducing a third variable, sometimes called the control variable, in the data analysis elaborates original bivariate relationships. For example, an initial crosstab might simply have looked at age and museum attendance. With a third variable, sex, we learn more about age differences which persist for both men and women. This finding suggests that age has a strong relationship since it endures within each category of the third variable.

■ ■ ■ ■ ■

BOX 2.3

NOW IT'S YOUR TURN

Here is some output from SPSS and the GSS. How do you read this bivariate table and what does it tell you about respondents' attitudes toward having sex education in public schools?

Sex Education in Public Schools* Region Crosstabulation

			REGION				
			Northeast	*Midwest*	*South*	*West*	*Total*
Sex Education in Public Schools	Favor	Count	80	126	124	79	409
		% within Region	89.9%	89.4%	75.2%	83.2%	83.5%
	Oppose	Count	9	15	41	16	81
		% within Region	10.1%	10.6%	24.8%	16.8%	16.5%
Total		Count	89	141	165	95	490
		% within Region	100.0%	100.0%	100.0%	100.0%	100.0%

(continued)

■ ■ ■ ■ ■

BOX 2.3 CONTINUED

QUESTIONS TO ANSWER:

1. Which are the independent and dependent variables and what are their levels of measurement?
2. What hypothesis is being tested?
3. Why is a contingency table suitable here?
4. Describe in words what the table is showing us. For example, what is the 24.8 in row two, column three? Put it into words. To get you started: 24.8% of . . .
5. Make a conclusion about the SPSS results using everyday language.
6. Can you conclude that there is or is not a regional difference here? What else would help you make a conclusion?
7. What could be plausible explanations for the results? Are there any theories or previous research that can guide you in interpreting the findings?

SUMMING UP CROSSTABS

Tables are an efficient and important method for presenting the relationship between two variables. In general, they provide descriptive information about a relationship between two discrete variables, typically nominal or ordinal level measures. They are often used with demographic variables and provide information about differences within the categories of those variables.

More complex tables can also be created by introducing additional variables, but these can become difficult to interpret if there are too many sub-tables to read. The introduction of a third control variable can help determine whether the initial relationship holds up under different circumstances or if it was a spurious relationship. For example, in the SPSS example in Table 2.6, a third variable of age could be included with categories of "under 30," "between 30 and 50," and "over 50." A table showing the relationship between rap music opinions and race would be generated for each of the three categories of age. By evaluating whether the same pattern found in the initial table still holds for each level of age, you can determine the role of age in explaining, eliminating, or reversing the original relationship between race and rap music opinions, and demonstrate how age interacts with race in explaining attitudes toward rap music. This method is sometimes called *elaboration,* or controlling for a third (or more) variable.

Visually inspecting a table can help you decide if there is a relationship between the variables and if some pattern is emerging, but to more accurately determine the relationship, statistical analyses should be completed. The next chapter presents crosstabs with interpretations of the relevant statistical measures.

CHAPTER 3

INTERPRETING
RELATIONSHIPS

Once a table has been constructed and visually analyzed for patterns and outcomes, statistics can then be computed to mathematically provide a quantitative analysis of the results. Sometimes our visual subjective inspections need more objective analyses. Making sense of the table and interpreting the statistics require practice. This chapter provides guidelines in understanding the statistics most useful for cross-tabulations and other bivariate relationships, in particular, chi-square and Pearson r correlation.

DEFINITIONS

- **Chi-Square (χ^2)** is a test that measures the relationship of two variables by assessing the significant difference between expected frequencies and those frequencies actually observed in each category of the relationship. It is considered a non-parametric test, that is, one suitable for data that is not assumed to be normally distributed for estimating population parameters.
- **Pearson r correlation coefficient** is used to assess how well two measures change together (covary), that is, whether the amount of variance in one variable is related to the amount of variance in the other variable. The resulting coefficient describes the strength of the relationship: those coefficients closer to 1.0 are the strongest and those closer to 0 are the weakest. In addition the direction of the association is indicated with a minus sign showing an inverse relationship and with no sign (an implied plus sign) showing a positive relationship.

ASSUMPTIONS

- Chi-square tests of significance are ideally suited for variables using mutually exclusive and exhaustive nominal or ordinal categories.

■ Pearson *r* correlations are for interval or ratio levels of measurement. Many researchers, however, use these correlations for dichotomies and for ordinal measures, especially if there are equal-appearing intervals. Pearson *r* correlations also assume a linear relationship between the two variables.

DATA FROM POPULAR PUBLICATIONS

Although many newspapers and magazines present tables of data, very few actually report tests of statistical significance. Minimally, a reader of data in popular publications should ask whether what is being presented represents a meaningful relationship, or statistical difference. For example, a survey conducted by the *Los Angeles Times* (reported April 24, 2004) found that young California adults aged 18 to 29 "were strongest in supporting the right of Indians to own casinos on their land, backing them 75% to 15%. Support tails off somewhat among people 65 and older, although it remains strong, at 62% to 31%." What the newspaper does not report is whether the difference between 75% and 62% is statistically different. Readers should ask if there is a significant relationship between age and support for Indians to run casinos. A chi-square test of significance would be helpful to assist our visual interpretation of these findings.

Too often writers and headline creators make a conclusion about a difference or suggest that a strong relationship exists between two variables (in this example, between age and support of casinos) without actually calculating statistics to back up their interpretations. A critical reader needs to ask such questions, particularly when the percentages and other findings among various categories seem to be very close.

A more likely source of statistical tests of relationships is an official report or study commissioned by an agency or business. Table 3.1 gives an example from a study conducted by the non-profit research organization, MDRC. In this report of high school "career academies" written in March 2004, the researchers were interested in seeing if these special school programs improved the students' labor market prospects and post-secondary school education participation, when compared to students not in the career academy programs, four years after graduation. Career academies are small learning communities that link academic and technical education with work-based experiences among local employers.

All researchers must deal with people who don't respond to surveys and fail to complete their questionnaires. One possible reason for the findings in a study could be that those respondents who participated are somehow different from those people who did not return the survey and thus they distort the outcome. The results from an MDRC report show whether

TABLE 3.1 Differences Between Respondents' and Nonrespondents' Background Characteristics

CHARACTERISTIC	FULL SAMPLE (%)	RESPONDENTS (%)	NON-RESPONDENTS (%)
DEMOGRAPHIC AND FAMILY CHARACTERISTICS			
Gender			
Male	43.8	41.4	55.2 ***
Female	56.2	58.6	44.8
Age of student at time of application			
13 or younger	8.6	8.7	8.2 **
14	35.6	36.7	30.5
15	46.1	45.8	47.2
16 or older	9.7	8.8	14.1
Race/ethnicity			
Hispanic	56.2	56.7	53.9
Black	30.2	29.3	34.5
White	6.4	6.5	5.9
Asian or Native American	7.2	7.5	5.6
Student speaks limited English	7.6	7.6	7.3
Student lives with			
Mother and father	61.7	63.3	54.3**
Mother only	28.6	27.9	31.8
Father only	4.6	4.2	6.6
Other family/nonrelative	5.1	4.6	7.3
Sample size	1,764	1,458	306

Statistical significance levels are indicated as: *** = 1 percent; ** = 5 percent; * = 10 percent.

Source: Kemple (2004)

those people who responded to the study four years after graduation are significantly different from those people who did return it. Both groups include people who went to the career academies and those who did not attend.

Identifying the Variables. The variables used to compare the two groups in this table are gender, a dichotomous nominal measure; age, an ordinal measure with four categories; race/ethnicity, a nominal measure with four categories; the percentage of students who speak limited English, an interval/ratio measure; and with whom the students live, a nominal measure with four categories. Five separate crosstabs are represented with five chi-square tests of statistical significance calculated, although the actual chi-square values are not presented.

Interpreting the Table. Chi-square is an appropriate statistical test to use in order to see if there are differences between the two groups, that is, to ask if there is a relationship between responding/not responding and age, race, language, and household composition.

Three of these five variables demonstrate statistically significant differences between those who responded and those who did not respond to the study. Women were more likely to participate than men: 58.6% of the total respondents were women, yet only 44.8% of the non-respondents were women. If the comparison groups were the same, we would expect both percentages to be similar.

Furthermore, non-respondents are older and less likely to come from dual-parent households than respondents. For example, notice that 63.3% of respondents live with both parents in comparison to 54.3% of those who did not participate in the study. Among respondents, 8.8% are 16 and older compared with 14.1% of non-respondents.

On the other hand, chi-square statistics were not significant for two measures. Those who participated in the study are statistically similar to those who did not participate in terms of limited English ability and race/ethnicity.

Making Conclusions and Explaining the Results. These data show that the sample of respondents is disproportionately younger, female, and from dual-parent families compared with those who did not participate. This difference may have some impact on the findings and make it more difficult to generalize the study to all those from the initial sample. It could be decided later on with more statistical analysis that the apparent differences between those people who attended the career academies and those people who did not attend them are the result of differences in characteristics of respondents and not due to whether they attended the academies.

There are many reasons why some people do not respond to surveys or follow up in a research project. Why younger women participated more than others cannot be determined from this sample, but comparisons with findings from other surveys and their non-response rates might suggest some explanations.

■ ■ ■ ■ ■

BOX 3.1

NOW IT'S YOUR TURN

As demonstrated in Table 3.1, in order for a comparison to be fair between two groups, researchers typically review the demographic characteristics of their survey respondents to see if there are any significant differences among various subgroups they are comparing. Ideally, the composition of each group is similar in order to control for any impact a characteristic could have on the outcome. In this same report of high school "career academies" conducted by MDRC, the researchers wanted to be sure that the comparison between those people who attended the career academies and those people who didn't attend isn't being affected by major differences in the composition of the two sample groups.

Review the following table and determine whether the respondents to the survey (given four years after their scheduled high school graduation date) who attended the career academies are similar or not to those respondents who did not participate in the academies, and how they both compare to the overall total. For example, 78.1% of all males responded to the survey compared to 77.3% of the males in the Academy group and 79.1% of the males in the non-Academy group.

Response Rates for the Four-Year Post-High School Follow-Up Survey for the Full Sample and Selected Subgroups

SUBGROUP	SAMPLE SIZE	TOTAL (%)	ACADEMY GROUP (%)	NON-ACADEMY GROUP (%)
FULL SAMPLE				
	1764	82.7	83.3	81.9
GENDER				
Male	773	78.1	77.3	79.1
Female	991	86.2	88.1	83.9*
ETHNICITY				
Hispanic	972	83.1	84.0	82.1
Black	523	79.9	82.2	77.1
White	111	83.8	79.0	88.9
Asian/Native American	124	86.3	84.5	88.7
EDUCATIONAL EXPECTATIONS				
Does not expect to graduate from college	614	82.6	81.8	83.5
Graduate from college	671	82.4	83.8	80.6
Attend higher level of school after college	448	82.8	84.8	80.7

(continued)

■ ■ ■ ■ ■

BOX 3.1 CONTINUED

Source: MDRC calculations from the Career Academics Evaluation Four-Year Post-High School Follow-Up Survey Database.

Notes: A chi-square test was used to evaluate difference between Academy and non-Academy response rates. Statistical significance levels are indicated as: *** = 1 percent; ** = 5 percent; * = 10 percent.

Source: Kemple (2004)

QUESTIONS TO ANSWER:

1. What are the variables and their levels of measurement (nominal, ordinal, interval/ratio)?
2. Why is a chi-square test used?
3. Describe in words what the table is showing us. For example, what is the 773 in the first column after the word "Male" in the second row of data? Put into words the very last number, 80.7. To get you started: 80.7% of . . .
5. Make a statistical conclusion about the findings. What does the one asterisk (*) tell us? So, what do you conclude overall statistically?
6. Put into everyday words what the researchers have discovered. Can they reasonably conclude that the two groups are or are not similar? Why should or shouldn't the researchers be disappointed that there are almost no statistically significant differences?

SCHOLARLY ARTICLE

It's the rare academic article that does not include tables of data along with statistical tests of significance. The goal is usually to demonstrate the relationship between two or more variables; chi-square and Pearson *r* correlations are commonly used statistics when analyzing data.

A. Pearson *r* Correlations

Alfred Adler was a noted psychologist interested in individuals' psychological birth order and the impact on their lives. He felt that as a result of various growing up experiences, people make decisions about their roles in the family. These perceptions then affect how they behave and react in life. To test this idea, Gfroerer, et al. (2003) studied 125 female college students by distributing several standardized measures. They then correlated the scores on the various measures to test their hypothesis that people's perceptions

TABLE 3.2   Pearson Correlations between Lifestyle Characteristics and Psychological Birth Order

BASIS-A SCALE	FIRST BORN	MIDDLE BORN	YOUNGEST	ONLY CHILD
Belonging/ Social Interest	138	−.372**	.307**	.005
Going Along	.112	−.339**	.018	−.220*
Taking Charge	.311**	.054	.106	.071
Wanting Recognition	.322**	−.132	.254*	.162
Being Cautious	−.178	.463**	−.301**	.270**
Harshness	−.197	.380**	−.193	.131
Entitlement	.094	−.225*	.476**	.228*
Liked by All	.179	−.007	.136	.139
Striving for Perfection	.439**	−.367**	.295*	.049
Softness	.085	−.470**	.265**	−.105

Note. $^*p < .05$. $^{**}p < .01$. Birth order categories determined by *White-Campbell Psychological Birth Order Inventory*.

Source: Gfroerer et al. (2003)   [Research Navigator: 9974951]

about their interactions with parents and siblings (called psychological birth order) relate to different styles of living (see Table 3.2).

Identifying the Variables.   According to the article, the *Basis-A Inventory* was used to assess such lifestyle traits as belonging to a group, going along with the rules, taking charge to lead, wanting to be recognized for success, and being cautious through a sensitivity to others' feelings. In addition, five measures were also used to describe people's background as possible explanations for their lifestyle traits: whether their childhood was particularly harsh or soft, how much entitlement to attention they need, how high a need they have to please others and be liked by all, and whether they strive for perfection and avoid mistakes.

Psychological birth order focuses on how people view their interactions with siblings, which may not necessarily be related to actual birth order. The 40-item Psychological Birth Order Inventory measured students' perceptions of their role in the family. Scores on this scale are used to understand lifestyle characteristics. Psychological birth order is therefore the independent variable and is an interval/ratio measure.

Scores on the various *Basis-A Inventory* scales are similarly interval/ratio and are assumed to be dependent on psychological birth order. Pearson *r* correlations are most appropriate to assess the strength and direction of relationships between interval/ratio scales.

Interpreting the Table.   Correlations have two components: the strength of the coefficient, which can range from 0 to 1.0 (where 1.0 is the strongest correlation) and the direction of the relationship, indicated by a minus sign (for inverse relationships) or an assumed positive sign. Significance levels are affected by the sample size; that is, weak correlations can be significant in large samples, while very strong ones could be statistically not significant in very small sample sizes. Therefore, the best guide is the strength of the coefficient. Roughly speaking, correlations below .2 or .3 tend to be weak, those in the .3 to .6 or so range tend to be moderate in strength, correlations from .6 to .8 tend to be strong, and ones above .8 are very strong.

In Table 3.2, for example, there is a moderate to strong correlation between those female students scoring as First Born on the psychological birth order inventory and their "striving for perfection" scores (.439). This value is statistically significant at the .01 level, although for correlations the strength of the coefficient is more important than the significance level. The profile of the first born appears to be someone who strives for perfection, takes charge in leadership positions, and seeks recognition.

Note that for the Middle Born, five of the seven significant correlations are inverse ones. This means that they are, for example, less likely to feel a sense of belonging or a willingness to go along with and please others. They also tend to perceive their upbringing as more harsh. Inverse relationships indicate that respondents who score high on one variable tend to score low on the other variable; positive relationships mean that high scores on one variable correlate with high scores on the other one, and low scores on one variable correlate with low scores on the other variable.

Making Conclusions and Explaining the Results.   Very few of the Pearson *r* correlations are particularly strong; only four are above .40. Yet they seem to correlate as might be expected from the Adlerian theories discussed in the Gfroerer, et al. (2003) article about birth order. We could conclude that there is some relationship between psychological birth order and how people view their lifestyles.

It's important to remember that these statistics are correlations between self-reported opinion scales and do not represent actual behaviors. Correlational studies demonstrate a relationship but don't tell us about causation. Given that respondents completed the various scales at the same time, it's possible that self-perceptions about lifestyle affected how they interpreted their roles in the family context growing up. What the study might be providing is a set of validity correlations rather than an explanation of cause and effect.

BOX 3.2

NOW IT'S YOUR TURN

Elementary school teachers responded to a survey about student-teacher interactions. The goal was to see if there is a relationship between the quality of the student-teacher relationships, and teachers' perceptions of their stress, negative affect/anger toward behaviorally difficult students, and self-efficacy in handling difficult situations.

Teacher stress was measured by creating an index using three items measured on a 5 or 7 point scale where high scores represent high levels of stress (item example: "Having to deal with behavioral problems in class, I have considered leaving this profession"). High scores on three other items (such as "I feel angry when a student does not follow directions") yielded a high "negative affect" score. Six additional items ("I have positive characteristics that are very helpful when there is a problem with a student") composed the "self-efficacy" measure. Teachers were also asked to estimate the percentage of students in their classes with whom they had "very good" to "very negative" relationships. The "very good" and "good" percentages were combined for a "good relationships" score and the "very negative" and "negative" ones for a "negative relationships" score.

Data from 113 teachers resulted in the following Pearson r correlation matrix:

Correlations Among Variables

VARIABLES	1	2	3	4	5
1. Teacher stress	1.00				
2. Negative affect	.48**	1.00			
3. Self-efficacy	−.45**	−.50**	1.00		
4. Good relationships	−.14	−.02	.02	1.00	
5. Negative relationships	.31**	.21*	−.11	−.57**	1.00

$^*p < .05; ^{**}p < .01$

Source: Yoon (2002)   [Research Navigator: *8768302*]

QUESTIONS TO ANSWER:

1. Which are the independent and dependent variables and what are their levels of measurement?
2. What hypothesis is being tested?
3. Why are Pearson r correlations suitable here?
4. Describe in words what the statistics are showing us. For example, what is the second correlation of .48 telling us? Explain the negative signs for some of the correlations. Why do some have 1.00?

(continued)

■ ■ ■ ■ ■

BOX 3.2 CONTINUED

5. Make statements about the individual correlations using everyday language.
6. Can you comfortably conclude that there is or isn't evidence to support the theories and goals of the research? In other words, is there a connection between teachers' self-perceptions on these three independent variables and how they characterize their good and negative interactions with students?
7. What could be plausible explanations for the results? Are there any theories or previous research that can guide you in interpreting the findings?

Chi-Square Tests of Significance

Chi-square tests are ideally suited to nominal and ordinal measures, as illustrated in Table 3.3. In this study, researchers were interested in seeing how 60 elderly women with chronic arthritis manage to care for themselves and live independently. Self-care is defined as the ability to perform tasks that promote one's own health. The research question focused on differences in self-care among those living in Long Term Care (LTC) facilities, Assisted Living (AL) arrangements, or living at home in the local Community. LTC is a much more controlled environment providing regular medical care and assistance than AL situations, which are residential facilities that provide assistance upon request.

Identifying the Variables.   Living environment is the independent variable with three ordinal categories: living in the community, assisted living, and long-term care. The researchers defined these as ordinal, based on the amount of independence each provided, with living in the community in one's own residence as the most independent compared with long-term care which is organized as the most controlled environment. There are 11 dependent variables representing different kinds of physical self-care and exercise. These are dichotomous nominal variables that are coded as reported by the respondent or not. Essentially, 11 crosstabs with chi-square tests of significance were generated.

Interpreting the Table and Statistics.   Although the actual chi-square values are not reported, statistically significant ones are designated with asterisks. For example, 63% of those in assisted living environments use a cane compared with 8% in long-term care and 37% in the community. These differences are statistically significant at the .001 level, that is, the probability of obtaining the calculated chi-square value by chance is less than one in 1000.

People living at home in the community use walkers and wheelchairs significantly less than those in assisted living and long-term care residences.

TABLE 3.3   Percentage of women reporting physical self-care behaviors and exercise by living environment

	PERCENTAGE OF WOMEN		
	Community % (n)	Assisted living % (n)	Long-term care % (n)
PHYSICAL SELF-CARE			
Splinting	37 (7)	25 (4)	12 (3)
Heat	58 (11)	81 (13)	64 (16)
Cold	21 (4)	19 (3)	8 (2)
Massage	63 (12)	75 (12)	60 (15)
Cane	37 (7)	63 (10)***	8 (2)
Walker	16 (3)*	56 (9)	60 (15)
Wheelchair or cart	16 (3)*	44 (7)	68 (17)
Other types of support	47 (9)	31 (5)	16 (4)
EXERCISE			
Walking	63 (12)	75 (12)	4 (1)***
Water exercise	16 (3)*	13 (2)	0
Exercise in general	89 (17)	88 (14)	68 (17)

$^*p < .05;^{**}p < .01;^{***}p < .001.$

Source: Baird, Schmeiser, and Yehle (2003)   [Research Navigator: 10953598]

Women in long-term care are significantly less likely to walk regularly for exercise while women at home in the community do significantly more water exercise. Other differences are not statistically significant.

Making Conclusions & Explaining the Results.   In 5 out of the 11 behaviors studied, differences emerged based on living arrangements. Along with other data presented in the complete article, the researchers concluded that there is some indication that where elderly women reside makes a difference in the amount and kind of self-care they perform to maintain health. Placement in long-term care facilities is often for those who have more difficulty in caring for themselves, so the findings make some intuitive sense. What this research does uncover is the specific kinds of behavior that vary among the three living arrangements.

▪ ▪ ▪ ▪ ▪ ▬▬▬▬▬▬▬▬▬▬▬▬▬▬▬▬▬▬▬▬▬▬▬▬▬▬▬▬

BOX 3.3

NOW IT'S YOUR TURN

In this study of 4176 patients with traumatic spinal cord injuries, researchers attempted to understand racial/ethnic differences in severity of injury and the source (etiology) of the injury. African Americans compose 90% of the minorities in this study. Paraplegia is paralysis of the lower half of the body and tetraplegia, like quadriplegia, is paralysis of all four limbs.

Categorical differences between minorities and non-minorities in terms of injury characteristics

VARIABLE	% MINORITIES $N = 1468$	% NON-MINORITIES $N = 2708$	χ^2	P
INJURY SEVERITY			7.4	< 0.01
Paraplegia	52.0	47.6		
Tetraplegia	48.0	52.4		
ETIOLOGY			953.8	< 0.001
Vehicular	25.2	48.2		
Acts of violence	49.4	8.5		
Sports	2.2	12.0		
Falls	17.0	22.8		
Other	6.3	8.5		

Source: Burnett, et al. (2002)   [Research Navigator: 7172028]

QUESTIONS TO ANSWER:

1. Which are the independent and dependent variables and what are their levels of measurement?
2. What hypothesis is being tested?
3. Why is Chi-square suitable here? Interpret the Chi-square test.
4. Describe in words what the table is showing us. For example, what is the 25.2 after the word "Vehicular"? Put it into words. To get you started: 25.2% of . . .
5. Make a conclusion using everyday language.
6. Can you conclude that there is or is not a difference between minorities and non-minorities in injury severity and etiology?
7. What could be plausible explanations for the results? Are there any theories or previous research that can guide you in interpreting the findings?

SPSS OUTPUT

Chi-Square Analysis

Should birth control be made available to young teens aged 14 to 16? Responses to this question on the General Social Survey were cross-tabulated with four age categories in Table 3.4 on page 64.

Identifying the Variables.   Because attitude toward birth control cannot "cause" age, it is dependent on the independent variable of age. Furthermore, Table 3.4 is set up so the categories of age each add up to 100% verifying that these categories are the independent variable's values. Attitudes are measured with a Likert scale which is technically ordinal but with equal-appearing intervals. Age in the crosstab is in ordinal categories ("age categories"), but the intervals are not equal, so this variable cannot be treated as an equal-appearing interval measure. Therefore, chi-square is a suitable statistic for looking at the relationship between ordinal level measures.

Interpreting the Table and Statistics.   Visually, it is evident that younger respondents (18-29) more strongly agree to making birth control available to teens. In fact, they are almost twice as likely as those 50 and over (40.1% versus 19.5%) to strongly agree. But are these statistically significant differences by age?

The Pearson chi-square test value is 61.4. The number itself does not indicate any particular strength or direction; it is not a correlation coefficient. It's therefore necessary to look at the significance level, here called "Asymp. Sig. (two-sided)." "Two-sided" refers to a two-directional or two-tailed hypothesis being tested, and "asymp" is an "asymptotic" distribution which is one way of mathematically calculating a significance level. A value of .000 means that the probability is certainly less than .001. It is the probability of the chi-square value occurring by chance when you have a table with this number of cells (indicated by a concept called "df" or "degrees of freedom," which is calculated by multiplying the number of rows minus 1 with the number of columns minus 1). In other words, the probability of obtaining a chi-square value of 61.4 by chance for a table with 9 degrees of freedom is less than one in 1000.

Chi-square is not a measure of strength. It tells us there is an association between the variables. To find out how strong the relationship is, a correlation coefficient must be calculated. Depending on the levels of measurement, different correlations are used. For example, to assess the correlation between two ordinal measures, a Kendall's tau or a gamma statistic could be calculated. Two nominal measures might use a lambda statistic.

Making Conclusions and Explaining the Results.   While these findings could be that one in 1000 chance event, we can still conclude that there is a

TABLE 3.4

CROSSTAB

			AGE CATEGORIES				
			18–29	30–39	40–49	50+	Total
Birth Control to Teenagers 14–16	Strongly Agree	Count	79	70	45	70	264
		% within Age Categories	40.1%	30.7%	23.7%	19.5%	27.1%
	Agree	Count	54	85	69	91	299
		% within Age Categories	27.4%	37.3%	36.3%	25.3%	30.7%
	Disagree	Count	41	38	49	102	230
		% within Age Categories	20.8%	16.7%	25.8%	28.4%	23.6%
	Strongly Disagree	Count	23	35	27	96	181
		% within Age Categories	11.7%	15.4%	14.2%	26.7%	18.6%
Total		Count	197	228	190	359	974
		% within Age Categories	100.0%	100.0%	100.0%	100.0%	100.0%

CHI-SQUARE TESTS

	VALUE	DF	ASYMP. SIG. (2-SIDED)
Pearson Chi-Square	61.408[a]	9	.000
Likelihood Ratio	60.387	9	.000
Linear-by-Linear Association	45.043	1	.000
N of Valid Cases	974		

[a]0 cells (.0%) have expected count less than 5. The minimum expected count is 35.31.

statistically significant relationship between the two variables. Attitudes toward teen birth control depend on respondents' ages. Remember, we are making conclusions about a set of respondents, not about any one person. It would not be correct to conclude that a particular 20 year old strongly agrees to make birth control available to teens. The table says that in comparison to other age groups, younger people are somewhat more likely to agree, not that everyone in a particular age group will agree.

Why is there an age difference? The data don't provide the answer but other variables in the data set might be used to explore the reasons further. For example, are religion, education, and political viewpoints relevant? Are younger people less religious, more educated, and more liberal than those over 50? Or is it because they are closer in age to the people targeted in the question? Maybe younger ones grew up in a culture more open about sexuality. This is where a review of the literature assists the researcher in making the appropriate conclusions. However, in no case can we reasonably make these conclusions without further data analysis. The answer about why there is an age difference cannot be explained by the table or statistics presented in Table 3.4.

■ ■ ■ ■ ■

BOX 3.4

NOW IT'S YOUR TURN

Do college grads feel differently about jazz music from those without a college degree?

Jazz Music (3) * College Degree Crosstabulation

			COLLEGE DEGREE		
			No College degree	College degree	Total
Jazz Music	Like it (3)	Count	539	194	733
		% within College Degree	48.6%	56.7%	50.5%
	Mixed Feelings	Count	270	101	371
		% within College Degree	24.3%	29.5%	25.6%
	Dislike it	Count	300	47	347
		% within College Degree	27.1%	13.7%	23.9%
Total		Count	1109	342	1451
		% within College Degree	100.0%	100.0%	100.0%

(continued)

■ ■ ■ ■ ■ ▬▬▬▬▬▬▬▬▬▬▬▬▬▬▬▬▬▬▬▬▬▬▬▬▬▬▬▬▬▬▬▬▬▬

BOX 3.4 CONTINUED

Chi-Square Tests

	VALUE	DF	ASYMP. SIG. (2-SIDED)
Pearson Chi-Square	25.523[a]	2	.000
Likelihood Ratio	27.860	2	.000
Linear-by-Linear Association	17.813	1	.000
N of Valid Cases	1451		

[a] 0 cells (.0%) have expected count less than 5. The minimum expected count is 81.79.

QUESTIONS TO ANSWER:

1. Which are the independent and dependent variables and what are their levels of measurement?
2. What hypothesis is being tested?
3. Why is Chi-square suitable here? Could a Pearson r correlation be used? Interpret the Chi-square test.
4. Describe in words what the table is showing us. For example, what is the 27.1 in row three, column one? Put it into words. To get you started: 27.1% of . . .
5. Make a conclusion using everyday language.
6. Can you conclude that there is or is not a difference here?
7. What could be plausible explanations for the results? Are there any theories or previous research that can guide you in interpreting the findings?

Pearson r Correlations

Many high school students, college admissions officers, and others interested in the role of standardized tests wonder at the relationship between course grades and scores on the SAT. Table 3.5 shows the Pearson r correlation results from almost 2000 university students.

Identifying the Variables.   Three variables are used in this analysis: total combined verbal and quantitative scores on the SAT (SAT_Tot), high school grade-point average (HS_GPA), and cumulate college grades (CUM_GPA). Each is an interval/ratio measure with SAT scores ranging from 400 to 1600 and GPAs ranging in this study from 2.0 to 4.0. Pearson r correlations are

TABLE 3.5 Correlations

		SAT_TOT	HS_GPA	CUM_GPA
SAT_Tot	Pearson Correlation	1	.184**	.161**
	Sig. (2-tailed)	.	.000	.000
	N	1870	1805	1637
HS_GPA	Pearson Correlation	.184**	1	.347**
	Sig. (2-tailed)	.000	.	.000
	N	1805	1919	1681
CUM_GPA	Pearson Correlation	.161**	.347**	1
	Sig. (2-tailed)	.000	.000	.
	N	1637	1681	1752

**.Correlation is significant at the 0.01 level (2-tailed).

suitable for studying the strength and direction of relationships for interval/ratio measures.

Let's now look at the various elements of the table. The first thing to notice in the SPSS output is that the top part of the table above the diagonal and the bottom part have the same coefficients. The diagonal is where the set of correlations of each variable with itself is located and designated as a perfect 1.0 correlation. Draw a line connecting the numbers 1 and you will see that the values above and below this diagonal line are similar, that is, the correlation of HS_GPA with SAT_Tot is .184 (row four, column one) as is the correlation between SAT_Tot and HS_GPA (row one, column two). Pearson *r* results in the same coefficient no matter which variable is independent or dependent. It is a symmetrical statistic and does not assume an order or causation between the variables. This table would not be printed in an academic journal as it is shown here; duplicate correlations are not reported.

Each cell also reports the number of valid responses for the two variables being correlated. For example, the first cell and start of the diagonal tells us that there are SAT scores available for 1,870 people (*N*) in the dataset. But notice the next cell has an *N* of 1805 which informs us that there were 1,805 students for whom we have both SAT scores and high school GPAs.

Coefficients range from 0 to 1.0 and are reported on the top line of the cell where the two variables intersect. They might have a minus sign to indicate an inverse relationship based on how the variable is coded or an assumed plus sign if there is a positive relationship. In this data analysis, all the correlations are positive. Finally, each cell reports the significance level of the

Pearson correlation, that is, the probability of obtaining that value by chance. Although the significance level can be less than .01, the asterisks, in the SPSS program only refer to the .01 level of significance in the footnote.

Interpreting the Table and Statistics.   The strongest correlation is .347 between high school grades and college grades. This is a moderate positive correlation indicating that those students with higher GPAs in high school tend to get higher grades in college. Another way of interpreting Pearson r correlations is to square the coefficient's value. This will allow us to evaluate how variation in one variable correlates to variation in the other variable. Here $.347^2 = .120$, or 12%. This tells us that 12% of the variation in the dependent variable is explained by the independent variable. This is sometimes referred to as a PRE measure, the *proportion reduction in error*. We reduce our errors in predicting or explaining the variation in our sample of college grades by 12% when we know the variation in the sample's high school grades. Obviously, 88% of the variation in college GPAs is explained by other variables, such as the amount of time spent studying, intelligence levels, motivation, difficulty of courses and instructors, and so on. You can see why a correlation of .347 is not particularly strong.

One of the limitations with Pearson r correlations is that when sample sizes are large, small correlations can be statistically significant. In this example, the probability of getting a weak correlation of .184 between high school GPA and SAT scores with 1,805 students is .000, which means $p < .001$. With correlation coefficients, the number itself tells us the strength and is often more important than the significance level. The correlations of SAT scores with high school grades and college grades may be statistically significant but they are not particularly strong.

Making Conclusions and Explaining the Results.   These correlations tell us that the better predictor of college grades is high school grades rather than SAT scores. Although there is some correlation between SAT scores and grades (those with higher SAT scores tend to have higher high school and college grades), these are generally weak correlations. Other explanations would be better at explaining or predicting college grades than SAT scores.

One explanation for the poor showing of SAT scores might be the relatively lower variability a college sample of students would have. To get into college, students should have higher SATs and high school GPAs, so the range of possible values on these measures is truncated in this sample. Perhaps if data across a wide range of high school students were available, including those who do not go to college, the correlations between high school grades and SAT might be higher. On the other hand, some researchers feel that SATs are not very good in predicting how people actually do in college courses.

■ ■ ■ ■ ■

BOX 3.5

NOW IT'S YOUR TURN

Is there a relationship between the age of getting married for the first time and the size of the family respondents grew up in (number of brothers and sisters) and the number of children they currently have? Here are data from the General Social Survey (GSS).

Correlations

		AGE WHEN FIRST MARRIED	NUMBER OF BROTHERS AND SISTERS	NUMBER OF CHILDREN
Age When First Married	Pearson Correlation	1	−.006	−.259[**]
	Sig. (2-tailed)	.	.831	.000
	N	1202	1199	1199
Number of Brothers and Sisters	Pearson Correlation	−.006	1	.202[**]
	Sig. (2-tailed)	.831	.	.000
	N	1199	1495	1491
Number of Children	Pearson Correlation	−.259[**]	.202[**]	1
	Sig. (2-tailed)	.000	.000	.
	N	1199	1491	1495

[**].Correlation is significant at the 0.01 level (2-tailed).

QUESTIONS TO ANSWER:

1. Which are the independent and dependent variables and what are their levels of measurement?
2. What hypothesis is being tested?
3. Why is Pearson r correlation used? Interpret the correlations.
4. Describe in words what the table is showing us. For example, what does a minus correlation mean (−.259). How would you calculate and put into words the meaning of r-squared?
5. Make a conclusion using everyday language.
6. Can you conclude that there are or are not significant relationships here?
7. What could be plausible explanations for the results? Are there any theories or previous research that can guide you in interpreting the findings?

SUMMING UP CORRELATIONS AND CHI-SQUARE

When reviewing tables of data that include nominal and ordinal independent and dependent variables, it is important to use statistics to guide the interpretation of the results. Although visually inspecting the data can show us what is going on, we often need the assistance of statistical measures to evaluate the relationship.

Chi-square provides us with information that judges mathematically the difference between what we have found in each cell of the table and what we expected to have found. It then tells us what the probability is of obtaining that chi-square value by chance, given the size of the table and sample.

Chi-square is not a measure of strength or direction, but a measure of association. When the probability of obtaining the chi-square by chance is less than .05, it is statistically significant (unless a more stringent level is set, such as .01 or .001). We could conclude that there is a relationship between our independent and dependent variables.

How strong the relationship is can only be determined with a correlation statistic. If the variables are interval/ratio measures, dichotomies, or at least ordinal measures with equal-appearing intervals (such as found with Likert scales), then a Pearson r correlation can be calculated. Coefficients closer to zero demonstrate no relationship, while coefficients closer to 1.0 show a strong correlation between the two variables. However, correlation does not indicate causation between the independent and dependent variables.

CHAPTER 4

EXPLAINING MEAN DIFFERENCES

In addition to evaluating whether there are relationships between variables, researchers are often interested in comparing two or more groups of people. Have the members of the same group changed over time or are there differences among the groups on some selected criteria?

One way of assessing differences is to statistically analyze changes in means. This chapter reviews several basic statistics that are used to explain mean differences, namely *t-tests* and *analysis of variance* (ANOVA, using the *F* test).

DEFINITIONS

- Independent-samples *t*-**tests** are mathematical ratios in which the differences between the means of a variable from two different samples (the numerator) are compared in terms of the standard deviations and sample sizes of the two samples (the denominator, or more technically, the standard error of the mean). The *t* value is then compared to a distribution of *t* values to determine its significance level. Roughly speaking, *t* values greater than 2.0 tend to be statistically significant, using a two-tailed test.

Paired *t*-tests are similar, but since they are used to compare one group on two variables, the mathematical calculations take into account the correlation of the two measures.

- One-way **analysis of variance (ANOVA)** is mathematically a ratio (the *F* value), comparing the distribution of values from a variable among three or more groups (the between variance numerator) in terms of the variance within the groups (the within variance denominator). Variances are deviations from the means, hence the use of ANOVA when comparing means. When there are greater differences between the categories than there are within the categories, we can conclude that differences in the means of a variable among the three or more groups being compared are significant. When the variances between categories are similar to the variances within each category, the ratio is around 1.0, resulting in a conclusion of no significant differences in means among the groups being compared.

ASSUMPTIONS

- *t*-tests are ideally suited for comparing *two* means ("*t* for two"!). This requires a normally distributed variable measured at the interval/ratio level that is compared between two categories (typically a dichotomous nominal measure serving as the independent variable). For an independent-samples *t*-test, the categories must be mutually exclusive, that is, no respondent should qualify for both categories. For example, when comparing freshmen with seniors, no one in the study should be both a freshman and senior at the same time. For a paired-samples *t*-test, the same respondents compose both groups, but each respondent must have two measures to compare. For example, subjects in an experimental study should all have both pre-test scores and post-test scores on some measure.
- ANOVA is best for comparing *three* or more means and variances. Variances and means require interval/ratio measures that are being analyzed for the categories of an independent variable, typically a nominal or ordinal measure. For example, college grade point average (GPA) might be compared among students from four different religious backgrounds.

SCHOLARLY ARTICLE

Changes in means and other data over time are typically part of many polls, newspaper charts, and reports from various government and non-profit research groups. However, they almost never present *t*-tests, ANOVA, or other statistical tests in materials available to the general public. Therefore, in this chapter, examples of the use of these statistics are drawn primarily from academic research papers and publications, rather than the popular media.

t-tests

In its simplest form, a paper could report a t-test in one sentence. Consider this description from the results section of an article (Mayo 2002) comparing exam scores from Introductory Psychology classes using case-based instruction (CBI) with scores from other sections in which college students are learning from a more traditional lecture format (Control):

Using data obtained from the 30-item exam, I undertook an independent *t*-test analysis to compare student performance in the CBI condition with similar performance in the Control. As hypothesized, student performance in the CBI condition (*M* = 83.23, *SD* = 10.29) differed significantly from performance in the Control (*M* = 76.76, *SD* = 12.43), *t* (134) = 2.34, *p* < .01.

[Research Navigator: 5655548]

This information says that students in the case-based classes (CBI) achieved a higher average grade of 83.23 compared with students in the lecture classes (Control) who averaged 76.76. Exam performance was more dispersed in the lecture classes (12.43 compared with 10.29 in the CBI format). This difference in means of almost 6.5 points is statistically significant at the .01 level as shown by the *t* value of 2.34 for this sample size. There were a total of 136 students in all classes completing the exam (as told by the 134 df, or degrees of freedom, which is the number of respondents in the CBI classes minus one plus the number of students in the control group minus one, or 136 − 2 = 134). The author concludes that the case-based method is an effective tool for teaching general psychology theories.

In its more complex form, a journal article might present a table of *t*-tests such as Table 4.1 in which reading ability test scores, spelling test scores, and scores on a measure of school behavior are compared between those students born in the months of May and June with those students born the previous July and August. The research focuses on students in their first year of school and seeks to understand if the youngest students in a class (those born before the June 30 cut-off date to enter school) are more prone to behavioral problems and lower literacy skills than the oldest students in class (children born in July and August).

Identifying the Variables. Three dependent variables are used: letter recognition test scores, word recognition test scores, and a measure of school-related behaviors. Each is an interval/ratio measure and suitable for the calculation of means. Students were asked to point to each letter of the alphabet and say what it was and to do a similar task with a set of words. Their scores

TABLE 4.1   Year 1 results: month of birth and literacy and behavior scores

MONTH OF BIRTH	LETTER RECOGNITION (MEAN SCORES)	WORD RECOGNITION (MEAN SCORES)	BEHAVIOR (MEAN SCORES)
May/June (group 1, *n* = 17)	17.68	14.765	20.24
July/August (group 2, *n* = 20)	22.1	21.75	32.55
Significance level (*p* value)	*p* < 0.008	*p* < 0.002	*p* < 0.000

Source: Menet, Eakin, Stuart, and Rafferty (2000)   [Research Navigator: 3788707]

were the number of letters they recognized correctly. An 8-item question-naire was constructed with a 5-point Likert scale for teachers to rate each student's behavior. High scores indicate very good behavior on such things as ability to concentrate, follow instructions, and general level of maturity. Two categories are compared: students born in May/June with students born the previous July/August.

The authors calculated independent-samples t-tests to measure the difference in scores between the two birth groups on each of the three measures.

Interpreting the Table.   Although Table 4.1 does not print the t-test values, they are discussed in the text of the article. The table instead shows the significance levels (p) for each of the variables. All are statistically significant; however, letter recognition test scores are not as dramatically different as the behavioral measure scores. It appears that the younger students (May/June born) are doing less well in letter and word recognition than the older ones (July/August born). Similarly, teachers rate the younger ones as having less good behavior, that is, less ability to concentrate, follow instructions, and work without supervision (some of the indicators on the behavioral measure).

Making Conclusions and Explaining the Results.   Based on these results, there appears to be some relationship between birth month (an indicator of relative age in the classroom) and literacy and behavioral success. The younger students in the first year of school are not doing as well as the older ones in the same class.

Why these findings occur cannot be determined from the tables. However, the literature review in the article demonstrates that other studies have pointed to age discrepancies within classrooms as a factor in differential performance and behavioral problems. Teachers may expect too much developmentally and cognitively of the youngest students by assuming that everyone in the class is at the same grade level regardless of chronological age.

Another t-test Example

A study of 2,429 workers with families focused on the negative impact of working different shifts on their families and on the workers' mood, energy level, and time. Table 4.2 presents some results.

Identifying the Variables.   "Negative Work-to-Family Spillover" score is the dependent variable, measured with five items, each on a 5-point scale where 1 = Never and 5 = Always. Items asked such things as "In the past three months, how often have you not had enough time for your family or other important people in your life?" and "In the past three months, how often were you not in a good mood at home?" These are interval/ratio measures so a mean score was calculated for these five items.

TABLE 4.2 **Multiple Comparisons (*t*-tests) of Negative Work-to-Family Spillover Means Shift in 7 Categories**

(I) SHIFT	(J) SHIFT	MEAN DIFFERENCE (I-J)	SIG	LOWER BOUND	UPPER BOUND
Evening	Day	7.663E-02	(NS) .962	−.1745	.3277
Night	Day	.2421	(NS) .172	−4.7270E-02	.4756
Rotating—changes each day	Day	.3210*	.001	9.814E-02	.5439
Split—2 distinct periods each workday	Day	.3755	(NS) .228	−.1111	.8621
Flexible—no set hours	Day	7.879E-03	(NS) 1.000	−.1670	.1828
Other	Day	.3014	(NS) .261	−.1022	.7050

t-tests treat one group as a control, and compare all other groups against it. *The mean difference is significant at the .001 level

Source: Grosswald (2003)   [Research Navigator: 12596307]

The independent variable was composed of seven different types of shifts, for example, the evening shift which can begin around 4 p.m. and go to midnight, or the night shift from midnight to 8 a.m. These are nominal categories so comparing mean scores between two of these shifts at a time requires an independent groups *t*-test. The researchers were interested primarily in how each shift compares with the standard and often preferred day shift. Another way of analyzing these data would be to compare the means for each of the shifts with one another at the same time; in this case one-way ANOVA would have been a more appropriate statistical method.

Interpreting the Table.   The table does not give the actual mean scores on the "negative spillover" measures. Instead it reports the difference in means between each shift and the day shift along with the significance level for the *t*-test used to test the differences in mean. Only one of the six comparisons with the day shift showed a statistically significant mean difference as indicated by the asterisk. The rest are not significant (NS).

The table also reports the lower and upper bounds of what is called the 95% confidence interval. This tells us that out of 100 samples taken from the population, the mean difference for 95 of them would fall in the range reported. Or in terms of inferential statistical interpretation, the true difference in means in the population is very likely to fall between the lower and upper bounds. For example, the difference in the mean scores between those workers on rotating shifts and those people on day shifts is .3210. However, the true difference in the population of all workers falls somewhere between

9.814E-02 (this is mathematical shorthand telling us to move the decimal place two spaces to the left) or .09814 and .5439. If 100 random samples were taken from the population, in 95 of them the mean difference would fall between .09814 and .5439. These confidence level ranges are usually not reported in articles, but this is one case where the researchers chose to do so.

Making Conclusions and Explaining the Results.   Only workers on the rotating shifts where schedules change day to day report the most negative impact on their families and their own energy and mood compared with day shift workers. People on other kinds of shifts were not significantly different in their negative impact scores from day workers. Perhaps these findings indicate that having a consistent work schedule makes it easier to plan your home life. Those workers whose shifts rotate and change periodically from day to night to evening seem to have a more difficult time arranging the routines of daily life with their families. Why this is so is explained further in the study with data analysis involving other variables.

■ ■ ■ ■ ■

BOX 4.1

NOW IT'S YOUR TURN

This study (Bisset et al. 1999) focused on comparing students, parents, and faculty in terms of their perceptions of the educational goals of a college education. There are six categories of goals (for example, personal and social development, science and technology) which are assessed with 34 statements using a 5-point scale where 5 is strongly agree. Independent sample t-tests were used to evaluate the differences in scores on these six goals between students and faculty.

A comparison of academic goals identified by students and faculty

	Group means		
	Students $N = 182$	Faculty $N = 62$	
A. Science and Technology	3.9481	4.3105	***
B. Humanities	4.0519	4.3629	**
C. Social and Behavioral Science	3.8615	4.2834	***
D. Intellectual Abilities and Communication Skills	4.4469	4.8172	***
E. Personal and Social Development	4.5775	4.6156	NS
F. Career Development	4.5407	4.2548	***

Notes: $^*p < 0.01$ $^{**}p = 0.001$ $^{***}p < 0.0001$.

Source: Bissetet al. (1999)   [Research Navigator: 2984074]

■ ■ ■ ■ ■

BOX 4.1 CONTINUED

QUESTIONS TO ANSWER:

1. Which are the independent and dependent variables and what are their levels of measurement (nominal, ordinal, interval/ratio)?
2. What hypothesis is being tested?
3. Why are *t*-tests suitable here?
4. Describe in words what the table is showing us. For example, what is 4.5775 under students for goal E? What does NS mean? What is the size of the samples?
5. Make a conclusion about the results using everyday language.
6. Can you comfortably conclude that there is or is not a difference between students and faculty in terms of the educational goals of a college education? What else would help you make a conclusion?
7. What could be plausible explanations for the results? Are there any theories or previous research that can guide you in interpreting the findings?

ANOVA

Comparing three or more means is a common goal in research. Consider Table 4.3 on page 78, which shows the relationship between self-image and ethnic identity among 347 Afrikaans-speaking Whites, 113 English-speaking Whites, and 466 Blacks in South Africa.

Identifying the Variables.   Using the standardized Rosenberg Self-Esteem scale, the author calculated two separate scores: Negative self-image (score range of 4 to 16 with a high score indicating a more negative self-image) and Positive self-image (score range of 5 to 20 with a higher score indicating a more positive self-image). Ethnic identity was measured with twenty 5-point Likert items and then factored into three subscales: (1) ethnic identification (such as loyalty to, respect for, pride in one's ethnic identity), with a range of scores from 9 to 45 with high scores indicating stronger identification, (2) achievement of identity and involvement with cultural activities of one's ethnic group (range of 6 to 30 with high scores indicating stronger exploration, achievement, and involvement), and ambivalence towards one's ethnic group (discomfort and uncertainty with membership in the group or the preservation and protection of the group's identity, with a range of 4 to 20 with higher scores indicating greater willingness to protect the group's identity and less ambivalence with membership in it).

TABLE 4.3   **Mean Scores and the Results of Analyses of Variance for the Various Scales**

Variable	AFRIKAANS-SPEAKING WHITES		BLACKS		ENGLISH-SPEAKING WHITES		df	F
	M	SD	M	SD	M	SD		
Self-image scales								
Negative self-image	6.66	2.39	9.21	2.89	7.35	2.89	2,921	99.47**
Positive self-image	17.49	2.08	15.97	3.31	17.30	2.29	2,921	32.47**
Scales associated with ethnic identity								
Ethnic identification	37.92	6.45	36.71	6.97	35.01	6.67	2,922	8.52**
Exploration, identity achievement, and involvement	22.84	4.76	20.73	5.64	21.13	4.43	2,921	16.79**
Ambivalence versus protection	15.36	3.33	12.64	3.65	13.42	3.14	2,922	61.71**

**$p < .01$.

Source: Bornman (1999)

All scales of these five dependent variables are interval/ratio measures and suitable for the calculation of variances and means. The three ethnic groups are categories of a nominal independent variable. Since means and variances are being compared among three categories, one-way analysis of variance is the appropriate test of differences.

Interpreting the Table.   The *F* values are all statistically significant at the .01 level. In other words, the odds of obtaining these F values by chance with samples of these sizes is less than 1% (one in 100 or $p < .01$).

For example, out of a possible 16 points on the negative self-image scale, Afrikaans-speaking Whites averaged (M) 6.66 compared with 9.21 for Blacks and 7.35 for English-speaking Whites. Differences among these three means are statistically significant. Note that the standard deviations (SD) for each group on the negative self-image scale are virtually the same, suggesting that the distributions of scores are similar for all the people within the groups. In short, variances between the means are greater than the variances within the groups.

The column labeled *df* is degrees of freedom and is typically reported in this format: The first number is the number of groups being compared minus one (2); the second number (921) is the number of respondents in each category minus one all added together (or the total number of respondents minus the number of groups). In this case, there are three groups, so the first number is two for each *F* test, and depending on how many missing answers there are, the second number could have been as high as 923 ($466 - 1 = 465$ Blacks, $347 - 1 = 346$ Afrikaans-speaking Whites, and $113 - 1 = 112$ English-speaking Whites, or $465 + 346 + 112 = 923$). These *df* numbers are used to determine the significance of the *F* value since it would vary depending on the size of the distribution. For example, an *F* value of 8.52 (for ethnic identification) might not have been significant if there were, for example, five groups being compared with 1000 respondents total ($df = 4, 995$). The value of *F* in itself is meaningless until a significance level is calculated, although values closer to or less than 1 are not usually significant.

Making Conclusions and Explaining the Results.   From these data, we can see that Black respondents had the lowest positive self-image and the highest negative self-image in comparison to the other groups, while Afrikaans-speaking Whites had the highest positive self-image and lowest negative one. Further statistical analyses show that the significant differences are not as great between the two White groups. (When *F* is significant other statistical tests are done to indicate which of the comparisons account for most of the differences, as the researchers did when you read the entire article.)

On the other hand, Afrikaans-speaking Whites scored significantly highest on the three ethnic identity measures and Blacks scored the lowest on two of them (the exploration and the protection subscales) but had no meaningful difference from English-speaking Whites on the ethnic identification subscale. The differences in means on all three ethnic identity measures are statistically significant according to the *F* test values.

Why these differences occur cannot be determined from the data presented only in this table, but becoming familiar with the long history of apartheid is a good place to begin seeking explanations. What is interesting is that members of out-groups often have stronger identification with each other and can demonstrate positive self-images. Why there are such differences and the reasons for a stronger identity and self-image among Afrikaans-speaking Whites are too complex to go into here. They are explored in the complete article.

Another ANOVA Example

Researchers were interested in understanding loneliness levels among a sample of elderly people 65 and older who participated in a community meal program. Results for 849 respondents are reported in Table 4.4.

TABLE 4.4   ANOVA Results; Loneliness by Relationship Combinations (N = B49)[*]

COMBINATIONS OF RELATIONS	M	SD	N
1. Not Married, No Children, No Friends	5.67[4,8]	3.26	58
2. Not Married, No Children, Have Friends	6.61[8]	3.23	66
3. Not Married, Have Children, No Friends	6.39[4,8]	3.33	169
4. Not Married, Have Children, Have Friends	7.49[1,3]	2.93	275
5. Married, No Children, No Friends	5.50[8]	3.81	18
6. Married, No Children, Have Friends	7.09	3.20	23
7. Married, Have Children, No Friends	6.75[8]	3.03	101
8. Married, Have Children, Have Friends	8.06[1,2,3,5,7]	2.99	139
$F = 6.56$ (7,841 df); $p < .0000$			

[*]The superscripts refer to a statistically significant difference ($p < .05$), using the Tukey test, between the reported mean score and the mean score of one, or more, other categories. For example, the mean score for category one is statistically significantly different from the mean of category 4 and the mean of category 8.

Source: Hall-Elston and Mullins (1999)

Identifying the Variables.   The dependent variable is amount of loneliness measured with an eleven-item scale, where each item is either 0 for loneliness or 1 for not lonely. Items were summed and lower scores represent higher degrees of loneliness (ranging from a possible zero to 11). These are interval/ratio measures suitable for analysis of variance. Typical items included "I wish I had a really close friend," "I miss the pleasure of the company of others," and "I experience a general sense of emptiness."

Respondents were grouped into eight categories depending on marital status, children, and emotionally close friends. This independent variable represents nominal categories.

Interpreting the Table.   For each of the eight relationship categories, the mean scores (M) on the loneliness scale, along with the standard deviation (SD) and number of respondents (N) are presented. Remember, lower scores mean more loneliness, so elderly people without children and friends scored the most lonely on the scale. Interestingly, both married and unmarried people without children and close friends were almost equally lonely in their scores, (5.5 and 5.67). Married people with children and close friends were the least lonely (scoring 8.06 out of 11).

The F statistic indicates whether these differences are significant. The first number (6.56) following the F is the value of the ratio. Numbers greater than 1 signify that the categories of the independent variable show meaningful differences in their means and variances. In parentheses are the degrees of freedom, calculated as the number of independent variable groups minus one (here $8 - 1 = 7$ followed by the number of people completing all items minus the number of groups ($849 - 8 = 841$). The probability of obtaining the F value with this number of categories and sample size is less than .0000 (certainly less than the usual cut-off level of $p < .001$).

The F test tells us that the differences in means among the eight groups are statistically significant. Because the number of comparisons made can be large, many researchers generate a post-hoc analysis to learn more about which comparisons are accounting for the significant differences. There are many statistical tests that are available with different assumptions for their use (advanced statistics books can explain these methods in more depth). The researchers here chose the Tukey test and the results are explained in the footnote to the table. It tells us that the small numbers next to the mean scores inform us which other groups are significantly different from that one. For example, the mean for group 4 (not married with children and friends) is significantly different from the means for groups 1 and 3. Notice that group 8 has a mean score significantly different from five other groups. Only groups 4 and 6 have mean scores not significantly different from the 8.06 of group 8.

Making Conclusions and Explaining the Results.   The data and statistics show that loneliness among elderly people is significantly related to the closeness of their relationships with spouses, children, and friends. In all cases, people with close friends are less lonely than others; people with children are less lonely than people without children; but married and unmarried respondents seem to have about the same scores. The best way to compare is to take similar groups in which one item varies; for example, compare groups 1 and 5, or 4 with 8. There you can see how similar the scores are and yet the only difference is the presence of a spouse or not. None of these mean comparisons is statistically significant.

Yet, compare groups 3 and 4 where only the presence of close friends differs and you can see that they are significantly different in mean scores of loneliness: Unmarried people with children but without friends are lonelier than unmarried people with children and friends.

Most research on friendships supports the findings of the importance of social networks, whether children or friends. But why spouses have less of an impact among this sample of elderly people is not easy to explain. The original article explores other parts of the study which might provide some insight to these findings.

■ ■ ■ ■ ■

BOX 4.2

NOW IT'S YOUR TURN

Researchers investigated how open new teachers are to use technology in the classroom. They hypothesized that the attention to technology would vary by personality type among a group of emergency permit intermediate and secondary school teachers. To measure personality type, they used the popular Myers-Briggs Type Inventory, which categorizes people into eight distinct categories. Four personality types are then constructed from these catagories. A 20-item Likert measure of technology was also developed to measure willingness to use technology; high scores represent plans to use technology.

Technology Scores by Myers-Briggs Type, Select Descriptive Statistics

Myers-Briggs Type	Number	Mean	Standard Deviation
Intuitive/Feeling	43	100.81	11.99
Intuitive/Thinking	23	105.04	11.47
Sensory/Feeling	30	91.03	13.09
Sensory/Thinking	63	94.76	16.11

Analysis of Variance, Emergency Permit Teachers' Willingness to Use Technology by Myers-Briggs Type Indicator

Source	SS	df	MS	F	p
Between	3491.85	3	1163.95	6.017	.001
Within	29983.86	155	193.44		
Total	33475.71	158			

Source: Chambers, Hardy, Smith, and Sienty (2003)   [Research Navigator: 10954975]

QUESTIONS TO ANSWER:

1. Which are the independent and dependent variables and what are their levels of measurement?
2. What hypothesis is being tested?
3. Why is ANOVA suitable here?
4. Describe in words what the tables and statistics are showing us. For example, what is the F value and p? What is the size of the samples? How do you read the means and standard deviations?
5. Make a conclusion about the results using everyday language.

■ ■ ■ ■ ■

BOX 4.2 CONTINUED

6. Can you conclude that there is or is not a difference between personality types in terms of using technology to teach? What else would help you make a conclusion?
7. What could be plausible explanations for the results? Are there any theories or previous research that can guide you in interpreting the findings?

SPSS OUTPUT

Paired Samples *t-test*

The General Social Survey (GSS) asks many interesting questions about what people like and dislike, including various types of music. Table 4.5 presents some findings comparing respondents' opinions about Broadway musicals and opera.

Identifying the Variables.   Opinions about Broadway music and opera are each rated on the same 5-point Likert scale ranging from "Like very much" (1) to "Dislike very much" (5). This is an ordinal measure but given the equal-appearing intervals typical of Likert scales, it can be treated as interval/ratio. Means in this sample of respondents can thus be calculated.

Interpreting the Table.   Opinions about both kinds of music were provided by 1,359 people. Because we are comparing their responses about opera with their own responses about musicals, and because each item is measured with the same scale, a paired-samples *t*-test is appropriate. Each respondent has given a pair of answers. We are not comparing two independent groups, but the same people on two measures.

On a scale of 1 to 5, where 1 is like and 5 is dislike, these respondents averaged 2.59 on the opinion scale about musicals and 3.48 about opera. The standard deviations are about the same and suggest similar dispersion of opinions for each musical type. In general, they seem to dislike opera more than musicals, although people seem to have mixed feelings about both types of music. Respondents are between 2 and 3 on the scale about musicals ("like" to "mixed feelings") and between "mixed feelings" and "dislike" (3 to 4) on opinion about opera.

The Pearson *r* correlation coefficient, reported in the second box, shows that there is a moderate correlation of .452 which is statistically significant for this large sample size. There is some relationship, yet r^2 suggests that only about 20% of the opinions toward one form of music can be explained by knowing the opinions about the other form. So perhaps liking or disliking

TABLE 4.5

PAIRED SAMPLES STATISTICS

		Mean	N	Std. Deviation	Std. Error Mean
Pair 1	Broadway Musicals	2.59	1359	1.098	.030
	Opera	3.48	1359	1.134	.031

PAIRED SAMPLES CORRELATIONS

		N	Correlation	Sig.
Pair 1	Broadway Musicals & Opera	1359	.452	.000

PAIRED SAMPLES TEST

		Paired Differences							
		Mean	Std. Deviation	Std. Error Mean	95% Confidence Interval of the Difference		t	df	Sig. (2-tailed)
					Lower	Upper			
Pair 1	Broadway Musicals-Opera	−.89	1.169	.032	−.95	−.83	−28.100	1358	.000

one type does not always correlate with liking or disliking the other. The *t*-test contributes additional information.

A mean difference of −.89 results in a *t*-test value of −28.1. The minus sign is merely a result of which opinion comes first in the table. It would still be .89 if you calculated the difference between opera and musicals, instead of musicals and opera. For a sample of this size (*df* = 1358), the odds of getting this value by chance is .000, which can be reported as statistically significant, or $p < .001$. A two-tailed null hypothesis was assumed: There is no difference in opinion toward musicals and opinion toward opera.

The 95% confidence interval tells us that if 100 samples were drawn from the population, 95 would have a mean difference between the lower and upper numbers reported in Table 4.5. In more everyday language, it suggests that there is a 95% likelihood that the true difference in mean opinions about these two forms of music in the population from which the sample was drawn is between −.95 and −.83 on the 5-point scale.

Making Conclusions and Explaining the Results.   The results suggest that although there are some shared "mixed feelings" opinions about both opera and musicals, there is a statistically significant difference. In general, respondents tend to dislike opera more than musicals and prefer musicals more than opera.

The data do not provide explanations for this. Perhaps other variables in the study could be used to elaborate on these results, such as educational level, social class, or age. We know that opera is a more difficult form of music to appreciate and understand compared with musicals, and the media images of opera are often negative. Perhaps these reasons explain the difference in people's responses.

Independent Samples *t*-test

Table 4.6 on page 86 gives more data from the GSS comparing the age of first marriage for men and for women.

Identifying the Variables.   Age is an interval/ratio measure suitable for the calculation of means. Sex is a dichotomous nominal variable. To compare the mean age of women's first marriage and mean age of men's first marriage, an independent samples *t*-test is an appropriate statistic.

Interpreting the Table.   The first box provides descriptive statistics (mean, standard deviation) on the age variable for the men and for the women in the study. The 492 men got married for the first time on average at 24.16 years;

TABLE 4.6

GROUP STATISTICS

	Respondent's Sex	N	Mean	Std. Deviation	Std. Error Mean
Age When First Married	Male	492	24.16	4.867	.219
	Female	710	21.84	4.929	.185

INDEPENDENT SAMPLES TEST

		Levene's Test for Equality of Variances		t-test for Equality of Means					95% Confidence Interval of the Difference	
		F	Sig.	t	df	Sig. (2-tailed)	Mean Difference	Std. Error Difference	Lower	Upper
Age When First Married	Equal variances assumed	.342	.559	8.066	1200	.000	2.32	.288	1.756	2.885
	Equal variances not assumed			8.085	1064.66	.000	2.32	.287	1.757	2.883

the 710 women averaged 21.84. Just by looking at these means, it seems that men marry later than women. But a *t*-test must be performed to confirm if the difference of 2.32 years is statistically significant.

The next section begins by first asking if the two samples are similar in their distribution of the variable. It would not be fair to compare the men with the women unless they were roughly similar in the distribution of ages in their respective samples. The SPSS output for independent samples includes the results of the calculations for two different *t* ratios, depending on which standard error formula is used in the denominator. To determine which *t* test to look at, you first must take a side trip and look at the Levene *F*-test for Equality of Variance (hereafter called the *F* value). If the *F* value calculated is significant ($p < .05$), then you conclude there is a difference and reject the null hypothesis of no difference in variances; equal variances are therefore not assumed. If the significance level for the *F* value is not significant ($p > .05$) then you accept the fact there is no difference and assume equal variances between the two categories. In the second part of the table, you can see that the significance level for the Levene *F* value is greater than .05 ($p = .559$), so you assume that the variance of marriage age for the sample of men and the variance of marriage age for the sample of women are approximately equal.

But the analysis still hasn't answered the question about difference in means. The Levene *F*-test was a side trip to figure out if there was a difference in *variances*. Now we have to decide if there is a difference in *means*. Note that there are two *t* values calculated: the one following the phrase "equal variances assumed" is 8.066 and the one following "equal variances not assumed" is 8.085. Since variances are assumed equal, we follow the *t* value in the first line and see that its significance level is .000, or simply $p < .001$

Making Conclusions and Explaining the Results.   We can conclude that the probability of obtaining a *t*-value of 8.066, with samples of this size and with these standard deviations and variances, by chance alone is less than one in a 1000 ($p < .001$) and thus statistically significant. There is a significant difference in the age of first marriage between men and women. Men marry later in age compared with women and women marry at younger ages compared with men. This does not tell us about any one particular couple, since the data are about numerous individuals, not couples or a particular person.

The data in Table 4.6 do not provide an explanation for this difference in age of first marriage. Cultural norms, tradition, gender roles, fertility and other theories might be used to understand at what ages people get married.

■ ■ ■ ■ ■

BOX 4.3

NOW IT'S YOUR TURN

Are homeowners younger or older on average than people who rent? Let's see what the General Social Survey uncovered:

Group Statistics

	Homeowner or Renter	N	Mean	Std. Deviation	Std. Error Mean
Age of Respondent	owns home	659	49.29	16.991	.662
	pays rent	322	40.28	16.942	.944

Independent Samples Test

		Levene's Test for Equality of Variances		*t-test for Equality of Means*						
									95% Confidence Interval of the Difference	
		F	*Sig.*	*t*	*df*	*Sig. (2-tailed)*	*Mean Differ-ence*	*Std. Error Differ-ence*	*Lower*	*Upper*
Age of Respondent	Equal variances assumed	.438	.508	7.809	979	.000	9.01	1.154	6.748	11.278
	Equal variances not assumed			7.817	638.8	.000	9.01	1.153	6.749	11.278

QUESTIONS TO ANSWER:

1. Which are the variables and what are their levels of measurement?
2. What hypothesis is being tested?
3. Why is independent *t*-test suitable here?
4. Describe in words what the various elements in the table are showing us. For example, what is the Levene's Test indicating? Which *t* value do we use?
5. Make a conclusion about the SPSS results using everyday language.
6. Can you conclude that there is or is not an age difference between owner and renters? What else would help you make a conclusion?
7. What could be plausible explanations for the results? Are there any theories or previous research that can guide you in interpreting the findings?

ANOVA

Television viewing is common among all groups of people. But is the number of hours watching TV per day dependent on some specific factors? Let's take a look at Table 4.7 on page 90 to see the relationship between highest level of education achieved and the number of hours per day viewing TV.

Identifying the Variables.   The number of hours watching TV is an interval/ratio measure suitable for the calculation of means. The five categories representing educational degree obtained are ordinal measures. Since we are comparing average number of hours per day among five independent groups of people, ANOVA is a suitable statistic to assess significant differences.

Interpreting the Table.   The first part presents descriptive statistics for hours of viewing TV for each of the five groups in our sample. For example, the 774 people whose highest degree is high school averaged close to three hours a day of TV viewing (precisely, 2.96). In that group, at least one person watched 0 hours (minimum) and another watched 20 hours a day (maximum). Standard deviations can be used to compare dispersion of responses around the means for each category and indicate how much variance there is within each group. The 276 people with less than a high school diploma have the widest range of responses (0 to 24) as indicated by the largest standard deviation. Can someone really watch TV 24 hours a day?!

Using just these data, we can see that people with the least amount of education watch the most TV per day, and respondents with the most education watch the least. To test whether these differences in viewing hours are statistically significant, one-way ANOVA is used. The value of F (32.3) is statistically significant at .000, or $p < .001$. This information indicates that the variances from the mean among the five groups are larger than the variances from the means within each group. Hours of viewing TV per day appears to depend on educational categories.

Note that the df for Between Groups is number of groups (5) minus 1, or 4; df for Within Groups is number of people in each category minus 1, added together for a total of 1481. A journal might report these data like this: F (4, 1481) = 32.3, $p < .001$. You can also see that the Mean Square number is the Sum of Squares divided by df (for example: 593.948/4 = 148.487). The F ratio is the Between Groups mean square divided by the Within Groups mean square, or 148.487/4.596 = 32.305

Making Conclusions and Explaining the Results.   Based on the significance level of the F test, we can conclude that there is a statistically significant difference in mean number of hours of watching TV among the five educational groups. Respondents with the least amount of education watch the most TV, while those with the most education watch the least TV.

TABLE 4.7

DESCRIPTIVES

HOURS PER DAY WATCHING TV

	N	Mean	Std. Deviation	Std. Error	95% Confidence Interval for Mean		Minimum	Maximum
					Lower Bound	Upper Bound		
Less than HS	276	3.93	2.820	.170	3.59	4.26	0	24
High school	774	2.96	2.137	.077	2.81	3.11	0	20
Junior college	90	2.63	2.564	.270	2.10	3.17	0	20
Bachelor	233	2.06	1.220	.080	1.90	2.22	0	10
Graduate	113	1.83	1.202	.113	1.61	2.06	0	6
Total	1486	2.89	2.232	.058	2.78	3.01	0	24

ANOVA

HOURS PER DAY WATCHING TV

	Sum of Squares	df	Mean Square	F	Sig.
Between Groups	593.948	4	148.487	32.305	.000
Within Groups	6807.252	1481	4.596		
Total	7401.201	1485			

These data perhaps represent an attempt at explaining why people watch the amount of TV they do. Education is a good indicator of this. But why is there some relationship between the two variables? Is it because of the amount of time more educated people spend reading? Or does the work that people of different educational levels do impact the amount of time they have for leisure? The data in Table 4.7 do not provide the answers; literature reviews and further data analysis can contribute more to explanations of this relationship.

■ ■ ■ ■ ■ ▬▬▬▬▬▬▬▬▬▬▬▬▬▬▬▬▬▬▬▬▬▬▬▬▬▬▬▬▬▬▬▬

BOX 4.4

NOW IT'S YOUR TURN

Here are some data comparing college grade point averages for students in four different departments.

Descriptives

CUMGPA03

	N	Mean	Std. Deviation	Std. Error	95% Confidence Interval for Mean		Minimum	Maximum
					Lower Bound	Upper Bound		
Psychology	129	3.2429	.39660	.03492	3.1738	3.3120	2.0	3.9
Sociology	87	3.2624	.40105	.04300	3.1769	3.3479	1.8	3.9
Political Science	79	3.1377	.37103	.04174	3.0546	3.2208	2.1	3.9
Economics	43	3.0540	.36729	.05601	2.9410	3.1671	2.0	3.8
Total	338	3.1993	.39345	.02140	3.1572	3.2414	1.8	3.9

ANOVA

CUMGPA03

	Sum of Squares	df	Mean Square	F	Sig.
Between Groups	1.799	3	.600	3.976	.008
Within Groups	50.369	334	.151		
Total	52.168	337			

(continued)

■ ■ ■ ■ ■ ▬▬▬▬▬▬▬▬▬▬▬▬▬▬▬▬▬▬▬▬▬▬▬▬▬▬

BOX 4.4 CONTINUED

QUESTIONS TO ANSWER:

1. Which are the variables and their levels of measurement?
2. What hypothesis is being tested?
3. Why is ANOVA suitable here?
4. Describe in words what the table is showing us.
5. Make a conclusion about the results using everyday language.
6. Can you conclude that there is or is not a difference in GPA among different majors? What else would help you make a conclusion?
7. What could be plausible explanations for the results? Are there any theories or previous research that can guide you in interpreting the findings?

SUMMING UP *t*-TEST AND ANOVA

Many research questions focus on comparing differences over time or across various groups of respondents. One method of analysis is to compare means, assuming that the variable being compared is an interval/ratio measure or an ordinal measure suited for the calculation of a mathematical mean, such as an equal-appearing Likert scale. It's important to remember that the mean is a summary statistic in itself and information is lost about a distribution of values when only a mean is used. Standard deviations describe more about the distribution. As was seen earlier, the statistics used to test mean differences take into account the standard deviations of the various distributions being compared.

If the comparison is between two mutually exclusive groups, an independent samples *t*-test is used to test the mean difference. When the comparison involves means on two separate measures for the same respondents, then a paired samples *t*-test is appropriate because it takes into account the possible correlation of the two measures for the same group of people (such as a pre- and post-test measure).

When the comparison is focused on three or more groups, one-way analysis of variance (ANOVA) provides an *F*-test statistic to determine whether the differences between the groups is greater than any variation that might exist within the individual samples. Comparing means is a common statistical technique and a supplement to information generated by Pearson *r* correlations or cross-tabulations.

CHAPTER 5

READING
REGRESSIONS

Answering research questions typically entails more than analyzing two variables at a time (bivariate relationships). Sometimes the focus is to understand how several variables work together to explain, predict, or describe a relationship with another variable. Multiple Regression analysis, sometimes called Ordinary Least Squares (OLS) linear regression, is a common statistical technique to assess the relationships among two or more independent variables and their correlation with a dependent variable.

DEFINITIONS

■ The **Multiple Correlation (R)** is based on the Pearson r correlation. R is a correlation coefficient ranging from 0 to 1.0 showing the strength of a relationship between a dependent (or outcome) variable and two or more independent variables. R^2 (sometimes referred to as the coefficient of determination) describes the proportion of variance in the dependent variable explained by the variance in the independent variables together. Sometimes the independent variables are called the *predictor* or *criterion* variables.

■ **Regression Coefficients:** *B* and *Beta* show the rate of change in the dependent variable brought about by each independent variable. *B* is actually the slope of the regression line used to represent mathematically the linear regression formula. The unstandardized regression coefficient (*B*) can be compared to the other coefficients only if the variables are in the same unit of measures. If not, the standardized regression coefficient, *Beta* (β), is more appropriate to use. These values communicate the direction (positive or inverse) and the weighting of the independent variable relative to the other independent variables in explaining the variation of the dependent variable.

ASSUMPTIONS

- Regression analysis assumes that a linear relationship exists between the independent and dependent variables.
- Regression works best when the independent variables have low inter-correlations or multicollinearity, that is, they are not strongly correlated with each other.
- Variables must be interval/ratio measures, ordinal measures with equal appearing intervals, or dummy variables (dichotomies typically coded 0 or 1).

SCHOLARLY ARTICLE

Although many marketing firms, political polling organizations, and other research centers make regular use of multiple regression analyses, these statistics are rarely published in popular magazines and newspapers. Regressions, however, appear quite frequently in academic journals and other research publications.

There are various models that can be used to explore the relationships between independent variables and a dependent variable. The two most common ways of testing the independent variables are the Enter method and the Stepwise method. The Enter method is used to test each independent variable in the order listed by the researchers. Each variable is then included in the final model, regardless of whether it is statistically significant. The researcher must then interpret the final model and determine which of the variables are statistically significant. Another common option is to use the Stepwise method, which results in one or more steps depending on how many of the independent variables are significantly related to the dependent variable. The program ceases when all variables are entered in order of importance, or when there are no more statistically significant ones to be entered. In this version, the statistical computer program does the work in deciding which variables are important in the regression.

The Enter Method Regression Model

Table 5.1 presents the results of a study looking at the reasons why counties in a particular state are more or less likely to support environmental ballot measures in an election. The data used in the study are not about individual voters; rather they are aggregated characteristics of counties, so the unit of analysis is a county. Although several states are studied, let's look at data for Michigan only. Notice that all variables are included, even those that are not statistically significant.

TABLE 5.1   Unstandardized and Standardized (in Parentheses) OLS Regression
Coefficients for Correlations Between Support for Each Ballot Measure (Across
Top) and All Independent Variables (Left Side) in Michigan, 1990–2000

	PARKS 1994 NE	HUNTING 1996 NE	WILDLIFE 1996 NE	BONDS 1998 NE
Population density	0.000 (0.00)	0.012** (0.28)	−0.005 (−0.21)	0.012* (0.22)
City w/50,000+	0.88 (0.05)	3.36 (0.18)	−0.59 (−0.05)	0.31 (0.01)
% Resource employment	−0.007 (−0.001)	−0.07 (−0.08)	−0.06 (−0.11)	−0.07 (−0.07)
Median income (in $1,000)	0.04** (0.40)	0.007 (0.07)	0.02* (0.36)	0.49** (0.43)
Education	0.22 (0.19)	0.56** (0.50)	−0.39** (−0.56)	0.35** (0.27)
% Republican	−0.10 (−0.10)	−0.20* (−0.19)	−0.14* (−0.23)	−0.12 (−0.10)
% Below 35 years old	0.25 (0.18)	−0.17 (−0.13)	0.12 (0.14)	0.17 (0.11)
Adj. R squared	.496	.566	.231	.643
N of cases	83	83	83	83

Note * $p < 0.05$; ** $p < 0.01$.

Source: Salka (2003)   [Research Navigator: 9750040]

Identifying the Variables.   The dependent variable is the percentage of
votes in support of the environmental ballot measure. The sampling unit is
the county, so in this table, votes are for 83 counties in Michigan. The ballot
measures are "Parks," focusing on creating an endowment to support more
state parks; "Hunting," prohibiting the hunting of black bears in the spring;
"Wildlife," giving control to regulate the taking of wildlife game to a com-
mission and out of the hands of a department or voters; and "Bonds," ap-
proving the creation of bonds to clean up contaminated sites and improve
water quality.

The independent variables are a county's population density, an interval/
ratio measure of the number of people per square kilometer (a smaller density represents a more rural county); a dummy variable identifying the
county with or without a city of 50,000 population or more; the percentage of
residents employed in resource related industries, such as farming, logging,

and mining; the county's median income, an interval/ratio measure; the percentage of residents over the age of 25 who have a college degree; the percentage of votes for the Republican candidate in the 1996 presidential election (Robert Dole); and the percentage of residents who are below the age of 35. All percentages are interval/ratio measures.

Multiple regression is most suitable for data analysis, given that the levels of measurement of the independent variables and the dependent variable are interval/ratio measures and the goal is to explain county variation in voting in favor or opposition to the ballot measures.

Interpreting the Table. Regression coefficients (unstandardized B and standardized $Beta$) and R^2 provide most of what we need to use. Although tests of significance for the regression equation (F) and the individual regression coefficients (t) are calculated by most computer programs, they are sometimes not reported in publications. The coefficients tell us the weight and direction (positive or inverse) of the relationship of each independent variable with the dependent one; R^2 indicates the proportion of the variance in the dependent variable that is explained by the combined impact of the independent variables.

The title of Table 5.1 tells us that the standardized regression coefficients are in parentheses. These can be used to compare the importance of the independent variables within each of the four regressions, that is, within each of the four ballot measures. The unstandardized coefficients are useful to compare each variable between the regressions. Remember that a variable's unstandardized coefficients (B) can only be compared with other variables measured in the same units (like population density for each of the ballots). Standardized coefficients ($Beta$) are best for comparing two or more variables that have different measurement units (such as median income and percentage of people under 35).

Except for the "Parks" ballot item, three independent variables are statistically significant for explaining support within each of the other three ballot regressions. For example, population density, income, and education are significantly correlated to voting in support of creating bonds to clean up contaminated sites. Using the standardized coefficients to compare the three significant independent variables, we can see the order of importance: income (.43), education (.27), and density (.22). Because they are positive coefficients, higher values for each of these measures are associated with more support of the ballot item.

Together, the independent variables explain .643 (R^2), or in percentage terms 64.3%, of the variation in the vote for bonds. Computer programs calculate an R^2 as well as an adjusted R^2, which is preferred when there are many independent variables.

Income and education appear to be strong predictors for three of the ballot measures. Note the negative sign of the regression coefficients for

"% Republican," which indicates that the more Republican votes in the county, the less likely there was support for the environmental ballot measure. Except for the "Wildlife" ballot item, around half or more of the explanation for supporting the ballots (R^2) is accounted for by the independent variables. For example, 56.6% of the variation in support for the "Hunting" ballot measure is explained by knowing the counties' educational level (Beta coefficient = .50), density (.28), and percent Republican ($-.19$).

Making Conclusions and Explaining the Results.   Education and income appear to be the strongest predictors for three of the ballot measures; political party and population density (rural/urban) are significant for two of the ballot items. In general, those counties with higher educational levels, higher income, more urban density, and fewer Republican voters are more likely to support environmental causes. For example, support of the "Hunting" ballot item came from counties with higher education, more urban density, and fewer Republican voters.

Regression analysis is a very good statistical technique for explaining and predicting outcomes. Understanding why people support or reject environmental issues is achieved with this analysis. But why education, income, urban density, and political affiliation correlate with environmental support may need further explanation. These data don't answer that question, but as you can see, each type of data analysis answers some questions while introducing additional ones for further research.

The Stepwise Method Regression Model

Another method of performing a linear multiple regression allows the computer program to select the statistically significant independent variables in the order of their importance. The regression procedure looks for the independent variable that most correlates with the dependent variable at step one, then searches for the next significant variable, if any, at step two and produces regression data based on those two variables. This continues until all significant variables are entered into the equation; the final step represents the best regression model.

Occasionally, researchers prefer to start in the other direction, that is, have the computer program include all variables at step one and eliminate the weakest ones at each step until the final model is developed. This "backward" stepwise method (available in SPSS) is used in Table 5.2, which shows the results from a study investigating how to reduce anxiety about computer usage among 86 teacher-education students.

Identifying the Variables.   The dependent variable is computer anxiety, as measured at the conclusion of taking a computer literacy course, by a 24-item interval/ratio scale whose scores could range from 20 to 80. The seven

TABLE 5.2   Summary of Stepwise Regression Analysis Using All Predictor
Variables to Predict Posttest Computer Anxiety

VARIABLE	B	SE B	β	t
STEP 1				
Computer confidence	−.93	.23	−.45	−3.96*
Computer experience	−.07	.17	−.03	−.39
Computer knowledge	−.44	.19	−.19	−2.31**
Computer liking	−.53	.23	−.24	−2.34**
Computer usefulness	.29	.29	.08	1.01
Locus of control	−.14	.19	−.05	−.73
Trait anxiety	.33	.08	.28	3.93*
STEP 4				
Computer confidence	−.87	.23	−.42	−3.84*
Computer knowledge	−.51	.16	−.22	−3.19***
Computer liking	−.45	.22	−.21	−2.10**
Trait anxiety	.33	.08	.28	4.22*

$R = .84$ and $R^2 = .70$ for Step 1 through Step 3: $R = .83$ and $R^2 = .69$ for Step 4. $N = 86$.

* $p < .001$. ** $p < .05$. *** $p < .01$.

Source: Rovai and Childress (2002/2003)   [Research Navigator: 8948093]

independent variables are also interval/ratio scales with high scores indicating how confident student teachers are with computers, how much they like using them, how useful they believe computers are for their work, how experienced they are (hours of usage per week, years of using computers), how knowledgeable they are about computers (none to substantial knowledge about networks, programming, and software), personality trait anxiety and more external locus of control on a standardized internal-external locus of control scale ("Many of the unhappy things in people's lives are partly due to bad luck"). All variables are interval/ratio measures and therefore suitable for a linear regression analysis.

Interpreting the Table.   The researchers chose to use the stepwise method of analysis but with the backward deletion method in which the weakest variable is eliminated at each step. Thus, the regression analysis begins with all independent variables at step one and proceeds to the fourth step at which point all the remaining variables are significantly predictive of the dependent variable.

The researchers published the first and last step only. You can see at step 1 that only four of the variables are statistically significant and by step four only those same variables remain. Because the value of a variable is affected by its relationship to the other independent variables, it is possible that a variable at step one could not be significant but then becomes so later on once other variables are eliminated.

The table shows the unstandardized coefficients (*B*), the standard error of that coefficient (interpreted similarly to the standard deviation), the standardized coefficient (Beta, or β), and the value of the *t*-test used to evaluate how statistically different the coefficient is from zero. The asterisks report the probability level for obtaining that *t* value by chance for each of the significant variables. Because these independent variables are measured using scales with different ranges of values (for example, the computer experience scores could range from 0 to 25 and the trait anxiety inventory ranges from 20 to 80), the standardized Beta coefficients are used to compare the importance of each variable in predicting computer anxiety.

The footnote tells us that at step one the multiple correlation (*R*) is .84 and the *R* square is .70, that is 70% of the variation in computer anxiety scores among this sample of 86 students is explained by these seven variables working together, even those not statistically significant.

By step 4 (steps 2 and 3 are not reported), only four independent variables remain and they together correlate .83 with the dependent variable, explaining 69% of the variation. Note how the values of the unstandardized (*B*) and standardized coefficients (β) change between the steps. If all four steps were presented, you would see changes at each step because the correlation of each variable with the dependent variable is a function of its intercorrelation with the other independent variables. Ideally, for regression analysis, the independent variables have low intercorrelations (multicollinearity). As a variable gets eliminated (or added in the forward stepwise method), the others then have to do more of the work in predicting or explaining the dependent variable's variation.

Notice also that the *R* square is virtually the same at step 1 and step 4; the three weak variables don't add much to the regression so eliminating them does not weaken the overall multiple correlation (*R*) or variance explained (R^2).

Making Conclusions and Explaining the Results.   The multiple correlation of .83 is strong and shows that the independent variables together explain a very large proportion of the variation in computer anxiety. In particular, compared to other students, teacher education students at the end of taking a computer literacy course who have less confidence in their computer skills, less knowledge about them, like computers less, and are more anxious personality types, tend to have greater anxiety about using computers when they begin their careers as teachers. Notice that three of the four variables have a negative sign indicating an inverse relationship between those independent variables with the dependent one.

Trait anxiety assumes a personality characteristic in an individual and this variable's correlation with computer anxiety makes intuitive sense. Similarly, it is understandable that students—even at the end of a computer literacy course—who feel less knowledgeable and confident and who like computers less than other students are the ones who feel more anxious about using computers in their classrooms once they become teachers. Clearly, the task in teacher education is to assist teachers-to-be with gaining more confidence and familiarity with how computers can be used in their new careers.

■ ■ ■ ■ ■

BOX 5.1

NOW IT'S YOUR TURN

A sample of 996 people completed a telephone survey on sexual behavior and marital functioning. Marital functioning scores are a summary of 10 Likert-type questions asking such things as how well things are going in the relationship, how happy they are, how often they quarrel, how frequently they kiss their partner, and whether they have any regrets about getting married. The nine predictive variables in the table focus on sexual behavior and satisfaction. The last item listed uses a nine point scale with higher scores representing satisfaction; the other items are based on True/False responses and measure respondents' opinions about their sexual behavior with their partners. High scores on these measures represent "True" answers.

The data were analyzed by age and sex, resulting in four regressions.

QUESTIONS TO ANSWER:

1. Which are the independent and dependent variables and what are their levels of measurement (nominal, ordinal, interval/ratio)?
2. What hypothesis is being tested?
3. Why is a multiple regression suitable here?
4. Describe in words what the table is showing us. Which variables significantly predict marital satisfaction for men under 60, women over 60, and so on? What percentage of the variance in the dependent variable is explained in each of the four regressions? What does the negative beta coefficient mean for the "not enough variety" variable?
5. Make a conclusion about the results using everyday language.
6. Can you conclude that there is or is not an age and sex difference here? What else would help you make a conclusion?
7. What could be plausible explanations for the results? Are there any theories or previous research that can guide you in interpreting the findings?

■ ■ ■ ■ ■

BOX 5.1 CONTINUED

Standardized Betas (β) of Multiple Linear Regressions Predictive of Marital Functioning for Men and Women of Both Age Groups Based on Items Regarding Sexual Behavior

	Under 60		60 or over	
Predictive variable	Women (n = 435)	Men (n = 368)	Women (n = 64)	Men (n = 116)
. . . sex act does not last long enough	−.03	.08	.19	−.09
. . . I do not believe I make love often enough	.03	.00	.11	−.14
. . . I am satisfied with my sexual partner	.15**	.05	.28*	.16
. . . good sexual communication	.18**	.17**	.23	.15
. . . not enough variety . . .	−.08	−.17**	.00	.01
. . . mutual fondling . . .	.09*	.09*	.04	.06
	Under 60		60 or over	
Predictive variable	Women (n = 435)	Men (n = 368)	Women (n = 64)	Men (n = 116)
. . . satisfying orgasm	.00	.08	.16	.04
. . . preoccupied with my sexual performance	.03	.00	.12	.03
. . . satisfied with your sexual relations	.35**	.28**	.06	.20**
R^2	.38**	.28**	.34*	.25**

Note. * = $p < .05$ ** = $p < .001$

Source: Trudel (2002)   [Research Navigator: 6810589]

SPSS OUTPUT

The Enter Method Regression Model

Not everyone goes to college, graduates, and moves on to graduate school in American society. In fact, most people do not have a college degree. What factors predict a greater likelihood of receiving more education?

In Table 5.3 are some findings from the General Social Survey (GSS) using a multiple regression model to understand and predict the number of

TABLE 5.3

MODEL SUMMARY

Model	R	R Square	Adjusted R Square	Std. Error of the Estimate
1	.612[a]	.374	.370	2.497

[a] Predictors: (Constant), Size of Place in 1000s, Respondent's Sex, Number of Brothers and Sisters, Respondent Socioeconomic Index

ANOVA[b]

Model		Sum of Squares	df	Mean Square	F	Sig.
1	Regression	2617.305	4	654.326	104.976	.000[a]
	Residual	4381.852	703	6.233		
	Total	6999.157	707			

[a] Predictors: (Constant), Size of Place in 1000s, Respondent's Sex, Number of Brothers and Sisters, Respondent Socioeconomic Index

[b] Dependent Variable: Highest Year of School Completed

COEFFICIENTS[a]

Model		Unstandardized Coefficients		Standardized Coefficients		
		B	Std. Error	Beta	t	Sig.
1	(Constant)	8.511	.455		18.704	.000
	Respondent's Sex	.384	.191	.061	2.015	.044
	Respondent Socioeconomic Index	.094	.005	.562	18.057	.000
	Number of Brothers and Sisters	−.132	.031	−.131	−4.255	.000
	Size of Place in 1000s	.000	.000	.059	1.952	.051

[a] Dependent Variable: Highest Year of School Completed

years of education with all the variables entered into the analysis in the order presented in the final box.

Identifying the Variables. "Highest year of school completed" is an interval/ratio measure asking respondents the number of years of schooling they have finished. Since we are interested in understanding what predicts or explains variation in the amount of education the 707 respondents reported, years of education is the dependent variable. The predictors or independent variables are sex, a dichotomous nominal variable (1 = male, 2 = female); socioeconomic index, an interval/ratio measure (based on education, income, and occupational prestige) for which high numbers indicate higher status; number of brothers and sisters, an interval/ratio measure; and size of place where respondent lives, an interval/ratio measure (a number in units of 1000). Interval/ratio measures and dichotomies are suitable for a multiple regression.

Interpreting the Table. The first box in Table 5.3 presents a key component of the regression model, namely, the multiple correlation (R) of all the independent variables together with the dependent variable. To determine the amount of variance in the dependent variable explained by the independent variables, R is squared (R^2). When there are many independent variables, the adjusted R square can be used, since it adjusts the R square for each independent variable in the model. An R squared of .374 means that around 37.4% of the variation in number of years of education can be explained by knowing respondents' sex, socioeconomic index, number of siblings, and size of residential place.

The last number is the standard error of the estimate, which is similar in interpretation to a standard deviation. It is a measure of the average deviation of actual scores from the predicted scores on the regression line. A small standard error of the estimate means fewer errors in making predictions.

The second box reports the test of significance of the regression equation used in the prediction or explanation of the data. It lets us know if the regression line fits the data and therefore if there is a relationship between the independent predictor variables and the dependent variable. An F value is calculated and a significance level is reported. If $p < .05$ (or, if desired, is less than another significance level such as .01 or .001), then we conclude there is a statistically significant regression.

Finally, and perhaps most importantly, the third box presents the actual impact of each independent variable in predicting the dependent variable. Unstandardized regression coefficients (B) are comparable for variables measured in the same units; standardized coefficients (*Beta*) are best when comparing variables measured in different units, as in the example here. Similar to Pearson *r* correlation coefficients, the direction (positive or inverse) is indicated by the sign, and the strength or weight of the variable is indicated by the size of the coefficient. These coefficients are technically the value of the slope of the regression line for each variable. To test if the coefficient is different from zero, a *t*-test is calculated and the significance level is reported. With stepwise regression, those variables whose coefficients are not significant at the .05 level are eliminated from the final model. However the Enter method was used here, so all coefficients are reported regardless of significance level. If the Stepwise method were selected, only variables with a significant regression coefficient would be included.

The first predictor reported is the "Constant," that is, the point on the *y*-axis where the regression line crosses. The constant is your best prediction of the value of the dependent variable when *x* = 0, that is, when you know nothing else about the independent variables. It is not normally used in presenting the findings, except if plotting an actual line or when using the formula to predict scores.

The coefficients for sex, socioeconomic status, and number of brothers/sisters are statistically significant (p < .05 for sex, p < .001 for the others) and size of place is almost significant at .051. We can see that socioeconomic index has the strongest coefficient (*Beta* = .562), followed by number of siblings (−.131), sex (.061), and size of place (.059). Together these variables explain 37.4% of the variation in educational level, as the first summary box reported.

Making Conclusions and Explaining the Results.   In words, we can say that those respondents who have higher socioeconomic status, have fewer siblings, are female, and come from larger cities tend to have more education. All variables, except the number of brothers and sisters, are positive coefficients: Higher values on socioeconomic status (more occupational prestige and higher income), higher on the "sex scale" (2 = female is higher than 1 = male in this study), lower on the number of brothers and sisters measure (fewer siblings), and higher on the size of place (more urban cities) correlate with higher education. Remember, though, that only 37.4% of the variation is explained; 62.6% of the variation remains unexplained. Clearly there are other reasons that predict higher levels of education.

We do know that women graduate from college at higher rates than men, people with more prestigious jobs and higher salaries tend to have had more education, and more highly educated people are likely to live in larger urban centers of the country. Perhaps the reasons why people with fewer siblings have more education can be traced to their parents' ability to afford higher education when there are fewer children in the family. What do you think? Explanations could be found in other questions asked in the GSS and might serve as a possible research topic for a paper or thesis.

BOX 5.2
NOW IT'S YOUR TURN

Here are some SPSS regression results (using the Enter method) from 762 college students analyzing the best predictors of College grade point average (C_GPA). Needless to say, many things impact how well students do in school, but consider these variables: High School GPA (HS_GPA), total SAT scores (TOT_SAT), rank in high school (HS_RANK), and Sex (1 = Female, 2 = Male)

Model Summary

Model	R	R Square	Adjusted R Square	Std. Error of the Estimate
1	.413[a]	.170	.166	.62220

[a] Predictors: (Constant), SEX, SAT_TOT, HS_RANK, HS_GPA

ANOVA[b]

Model		Sum of Squares	df	Mean Square	F	Sig.
1	Regression	60.184	4	15.046	38.865	.000[a]
	Residual	293.446	758	.387		
	Total	353.630	762			

[a] Predictors: (Constant), SEX, SAT_TOT, HS_RANK, HS_GPA

[b] Dependent Variable: C_GPA

Coefficients[a]

Model		Unstandardized Coefficients		Standardized Coefficients		
		B	Std. Error	Beta	t	Sig.
1	(Constant)	1.137	.333		3.414	.001
	HS_GPA	.378	.074	.262	5.123	.000
	HS_RANK	−.016	.019	−.042	−.841	.401
	SAT_TOT	.001	.000	.157	4.546	.000
	SEX	−.226	.048	−.162	−4.727	.000

[a] Dependent Variable: C_GPA

(continued)

■ ■ ■ ■ ■

BOX 5.2 CONTINUED

QUESTIONS TO ANSWER:

1. Which are the independent and dependent variables and what are their levels of measurement?
2. What hypothesis is being tested?
3. Why is a multiple regression suitable here?
4. Describe in words what the table is showing us. What is R and R squared? What does the F test tell us about the regression? Which variables are good predictors of the dependent variable? What is the difference between B and *Beta* and why do some have negative signs?
5. Make a conclusion about the results using everyday language.
6. Can you conclude that there is or is not a relationship between the independent and dependent variables? What else would help you make a conclusion?
7. What could be plausible explanations for the results? Are there any theories or previous research that can guide you in interpreting the findings?

The Stepwise Method Regression

Sometimes we may not have an idea or theory about which independent variables might be related to the dependent variable. In these cases, a stepwise multiple regression would provide a way to explore which ones are most relevant and how they interact with each other.

Consider the example in Table 5.4 which attempts to understand why people vary in the number of children they have.

TABLE 5.4

MODEL SUMMARY

Model	R	R Square	Adjusted R Square	Std. Error of the Estimate
1	.301[a]	.091	.089	1.511
2	.412[b]	.170	.167	1.446
3	.438[c]	.191	.187	1.428

[a] Predictors: (Constant), Age of Respondent

[b] Predictors: (Constant), Age of Respondent, Age When First Married

[c] Predictors: (Constant), Age of Respondent, Age When First Married, Number of Brothers and Sisters

(continued)

TABLE 5.4 (CONTINUED)

ANOVA[d]

Model		Sum of Squares	df	Mean Square	F	Sig.
1	Regression	138.801	1	138.801	60.767	.000[a]
	Residual	1388.755	608	2.284		
	Total	1527.556	609			
2	Regression	259.206	2	129.603	62.025	.000[b]
	Residual	1268.350	607	2.090		
	Total	1527.556	609			
3	Regression	292.450	3	97.483	47.830	.000[c]
	Residual	1235.105	606	2.038		
	Total	1527.556	609			

[a] Predictors: (Constant), Age of Respondent
[b] Predictors: (Constant), Age of Respondent, Age When First Married
[c] Predictors: (Constant), Age of Respondent, Age When First Married, Number of Brothers and Sisters
[d] Dependent Variable: Number of Children

COEFFICIENTS[a]

Model		Unstandardized Coefficients		Standardized Coefficients		
		B	Std. Error	Beta	t	Sig.
1	(Constant)	.805	.197		4.095	.000
	Age of Respondent	.029	.004	.301	7.795	.000
2	(Constant)	2.719	.315		8.645	.000
	Age of Respondent	.031	.004	.332	8.931	.000
	Age When First Married	−.090	.012	−.282	−7.591	.000
3	(Constant)	2.491	.316		7.887	.000
	Age of Respondent	.030	.003	.315	8.530	.000
	Age When First Married	−.089	.012	−.279	−7.598	.000
	Number of Brothers and Sisters	.072	.018	.148	4.039	.000

[a] Dependent Variable: Number of Children

(continued)

TABLE 5.4 (CONTINUED)

EXCLUDED VARIABLES[d]

Model		Beta In	t	Sig.	Partial Correlation	Collinearity Statistics
						Tolerance
1	Number of Brothers and Sisters	.154[a]	4.018	.000	.161	.988
	Highest Year of School Completed	−.136[a]	−3.381	.001	−.136	.904
	Age When First Married	−.282[a]	−7.591	.000	−.294	.988
	Size of Place in 1000s	−.046[a]	−1.190	.234	−.048	1.000
2	Number of Brothers and Sisters	.148[b]	4.039	.000	.162	.987
	Highest Year of School Completed	−.067[b]	−1.675	.094	−.068	.849
	Size of Place in 1000s	−.039[b]	−1.065	.287	−.043	.999
3	Highest Year of School Completed	−.027[c]	−.665	.507	−.027	.791
	Size of Place in 1000s	−.034[c]	−.923	.356	−.037	.998

[a] Predictors in the Model: (Constant), Age of Respondent

[b] Predictors in the Model: (Constant), Age of Respondent, Age When First Married

[c] Predictors in the Model: (Constant), Age of Respondent, Age When First Married, Number of Brothers and Sisters

[d] Dependent Variable: Number of Children

Identifying the Variables.   Number of children is a discrete interval/ratio measure, although the last category represents eight or more children. But given how few have that many children, the variable is essentially an interval/ratio one and suitable for a regression. The independent variables—age of respondent, age at first marriage, and number of siblings—similarly are all interval/ratio measures that can be used in a regression analysis.

Interpreting the Table. Four sections are presented, which summarize the stepwise regression analysis. The first part is an important summary of the multiple correlations (R) and R squares at each step of the analysis. Note that there are three steps (or models) in this example. At step one, the value of R is .301 but it reaches .438 by the last step. Change in R square goes from approximately 9% to 19%. Clearly, step 3 presents a more complete picture of the relationship between the independent variables and the dependent one; adding additional variables increases the explanation of the dependent variable.

The second section shows the ANOVA used to test the significance of the regression models at each step. With significance levels for the F value at .000, the regression equations generated at each step are statistically significant at $p < .001$. Usually this information is not reported in an article; it is there to guide the researcher in verifying the significance of the regression analysis.

The third section presents the standardized ($Beta$) and unstandardized (B) coefficients for the independent variables, along with the t-test results analyzing how different these coefficients are from zero. Three models are presented, one at each step of the analysis. The important one is the last one, when all the significant variables have been entered. Compare these sets of data with the fourth section, Excluded Variables, which presents the coefficients for the variables that are not entered at each step.

For example, at step 1, age of respondent enters the equation as the strongest variable in predicting number of children. It has a beta coefficient of .301 (standardized coefficients are better to use here since the variables cannot be compared—number of children and age of first marriage, for example, have different units). Compare the value of .301 with the beta coefficients at step 1 in the Excluded Variables table and you can see it is the highest one. You can also see that the variable in the Excluded Variable step 1 with the highest value and statistical significance is age of first marriage, so it is likely to enter the regression at step 2.

Sure enough at step 2, we can now see that age of first marriage has entered the regression with a value of −.282 (the negative sign does not make it smaller; it is the direction of the relationship, not its strength). Also note that the beta coefficient for age of respondent has changed. Remember these coefficients are based on the combined effect of both independent variables at the same time in explaining the dependent variable. By itself, age of respondent correlated with number of children at .301; included with age of first marriage, age of respondent now correlates with number of children at .332.

Now go back to the summary table in the first section: You can see that age of respondent and age of first marriage *together* correlate with number of children at .412. Working with one another, these two independent variables do more to explain number of children than either one does by itself.

Finally, at step 3, number of brothers and sisters enters the regression analysis. Notice it had the highest coefficient at step 2 of the Excluded Variables and was the only one statistically significant at that stage, so it was a likely candidate to enter at step 3. The other information in the Excluded Variables section provides what is called the partial correlation (the correlation of that variable while holding the other ones constant, or its unique contribution to the correlation), and other information suited to more advanced statistical analyses. At step 3, you can see which variables remain excluded. They do not have statistically significant beta coefficients to enter the regression. In other words, they have little impact in explaining or predicting the dependent variable.

The final step (3) in the Coefficients section plus the summary information at step 3 in the first part of the output are the most important ones since they provide the information about which variables contribute to the regression analysis and how strongly. By comparing *beta* coefficients (or the unstandardized *B* coefficients in the cases where all the variables are measured using the same scale), we can see that age of respondent, age of first marriage, and number of brothers and sisters, in that order, correlate with the number of children they have. Refer to step 3 of the summary table in the first part to see that the three variables together correlate .438 and explain 19.1% of the variation in the dependent variable.

In short, the key information from an SPSS stepwise regression output can be found in the last steps of the Model Summary and Coefficients sections. There the value of the coefficients and their combined multiple correlation with the dependent variable are reported. Most researchers report the beta weights for each variable, the value of *R*, and *R* square.

Making Conclusions and Explaining the Results.   These results tell us that the reasons why respondents have different numbers of children can be explained by looking at their current age, the age they first got married, and the number of brothers and sisters they have. Specifically, those respondents with more children, compared to those respondents with fewer children, tend to be older, got married at younger ages, and have more siblings. The negative sign for age of first marriage tells us this is an inverse relationship: Fewer children is correlated with later age of first marriage, and more children with earlier age of marriage.

These findings make sense since those respondents who get married at younger ages and are older have had more time to have children. Additionally, perhaps, people from earlier generations tended to have larger families, so older respondents reflect that difference as well. Add in the somewhat good correlation between having many siblings and having many children, we can predict the number of children people have by knowing these three things about them. Yet, together they explain about 19% of the variation, leaving a residual of 81% unexplained. Clearly there are other reasons why different people have different numbers of children. Other variables, guided by theory and previous research, can be included in another regression analysis. Educational level and size of hometown (an indicator of urban or rural living) did not seem relevant, so other measures must be investigated, perhaps income level, occupational choice, race/ethnicity, religion, and other possible explanations.

■ ■ ■ ■ ■

BOX 5.3

NOW IT'S YOUR TURN

Here are some SPSS regression results (using the Stepwise method) from the General Social Survey. It attempts to understand differences between liberals and conservatives. Political view is coded as 1 = extremely liberal to 7 = extremely conservative; married is coded with 1 = yes, 2 = no; sex is coded 1 = male, 2 = female; and size of place is measured in number of people in respondents' hometown.

Model Summary

Model	R	R Square	Adjusted R Square	Std. Error of the Estimate
1	.127(a)	.016	.015	1.356
2	.168(b)	.028	.026	1.349
3	.195(c)	.038	.034	1.343

[a] Predictors: (Constant), Size of Place in 1000s

[b] Predictors: (Constant), Size of Place in 1000s, Age of Respondent

[c] Predictors: (Constant), Size of Place in 1000s, Age of Respondent, Married?

ANOVA[d]

Model		Sum of Squares	df	Mean Square	F	Sig.
1	Regression	21.823	1	21.823	11.863	.001[a]
	Residual	1320.822	718	1.840		
	Total	1342.644	719			
2	Regression	37.977	2	18.989	10.435	.000[b]
	Residual	1304.667	717	1.820		
	Total	1342.644	719			
3	Regression	50.929	3	16.976	9.410	.000[c]
	Residual	1291.716	716	1.804		
	Total	1342.644	719			

(continued)

■ ■ ■ ■ ■

BOX 5.3 CONTINUED

[a] Predictors: (Constant), Size of Place in 1000s

[b] Predictors: (Constant), Size of Place in 1000s, Age of Respondent

[c] Predictors: (Constant), Size of Place in 1000s, Age of Respondent, Married?

[d] Dependent Variable: Think of Self as Liberal or Conservative

Coefficients[a]

Model		Unstandardized Coefficients		Standardized Coefficients		
		B	Std. Error	Beta	t	Sig.
1	(Constant)	4.280	.053		81.101	.000
	Size of Place in 1000s	.000	.000	−.127	−3.444	.001
2	(Constant)	3.873	.146		26.463	.000
	Size of Place in 1000s	.000	.000	−.124	−3.376	.001
	Age of Respondent	.009	.003	.110	2.980	.003
3	(Constant)	4.254	.204		20.891	.000
	Size of Place in 1000s	.000	.000	−.117	−3.170	.002
	Age of Respondent	.009	.003	.112	3.056	.002
	Married?	−.270	.101	−.099	−2.679	.008

[a] Dependent Variable: Think of Self as Liberal or Conservative

(continued)

■ ■ ■ ■ ■

BOX 5.3 CONTINUED

Excluded Variables[d]

Model		Beta In	t	Sig.	Partial Correlation	Collinearity Statistics Tolerance
1	Highest Year of School Completed	−.082[a]	−2.205	.028	−.082	.996
	Age of Respondent	.110[a]	2.980	.003	.111	.999
	Married?	−.096[a]	−2.592	.010	−.096	.994
	Respondent's Sex	−.030[a]	−.799	.424	−.030	.998
2	Highest Year of School Completed	−.057[b]	−1.508	.132	−.056	.932
	Married?	−.099[b]	−2.679	.008	−.100	.993
	Respondent's Sex	−.034[b]	−.928	.354	−.035	.996
3	Highest Year of School Completed	−.069[c]	−1.815	.070	−.068	.921
	Respondent's Sex	−.023[c]	−.622	.534	−.023	.982

[a] Predictors in the Model: (Constant), Size of Place in 1000s

[b] Predictors in the Model: (Constant), Size of Place in 1000s, Age of Respondent

[c] Predictors in the Model: (Constant), Size of Place in 1000s, Age of Respondent, Married?

[d] Dependent Variable: Think of Self as Liberal or Conservative

QUESTIONS TO ANSWER:

1. Which are the independent and dependent variables and what are their levels of measurement?
2. What hypothesis is being tested?
3. Why is a multiple regression suitable here?
4. Describe in words what the table is showing us. What is R and R squared? What is meant by the three numbered models? Which do you look at? Which variables are good predictors of the dependent variable? What is the difference between B and *Beta* and why do some have negative signs?
5. What do the data in the Excluded Variables section tell us?
6. Make a conclusion about the results using everyday language.
7. Can you conclude that there is or is not a relationship between the independent and dependent variables? What else would help you make a conclusion?
8. What could be plausible explanations for the results? Are there any theories or previous research that can guide you in interpreting the findings?

SUMMING UP REGRESSIONS

A very common analysis in social science research is the use of ordinary least squares regression, often called multiple regression. Its goal is to predict or explain variation in a dependent variable with two or more independent variables. These variables must be assumed to have a linear relationship with the dependent variable and have low intercorrelations with each other.

Key to interpreting this statistical procedure is to focus on the value of R (the multiple correlation), R^2 (R square), and the direction and size of the regression coefficients (unstandardized B or standardized $Beta$). If using the stepwise method, the information needed is given in the last model in each section of the table. The Excluded Variables section lists the variables that are not statistically significant in predicting or explaining the dependent variable.

However, if the overall regression model is not statistically significant (the F value in the ANOVA provides this information), then it is very likely that none of the independent variables is significantly predicting the dependent variable. The larger the R square, the more variation in the dependent variable being explained or predicted by the independent variables. The values of the regression coefficients describe how much work each independent variable is contributing to the prediction. Higher value coefficients are doing most of the work.

CREDITS AND REFERENCES

Auton, Heather R., Jacqueline Pope, and Gus Seeger. 2003. "It Isn't That Strange: Paranormal Belief and Personality Traits." *Social Behavior and Personality* 31:7, 711–720. Table used by permission of *Social Behavior and Personality*.

Baird, Carol L., Donna Schmeiser, and Karen T. Yehle. 2003. "Self-Caring of Women with Osteoarthritis Living at Different Levels of Independence." *Health Care for Women International* 24, 617–634. Table Copyright © 2003 by Baird, et al. and reproduced by permission of Taylor & Francis, Inc. http://www.taylorandfrancis.com.

Bisset, Janet D., Marianne E. Borja, Deborah E. Brassard, Janet R. Reohr, Kathleen O'Neill, and Kathleen O'Neill Ruthkosky. 1999. "Assessing the Importance of Educational Goals: A Comparison of Students, Faculty, and Parents." *Assessment & Evaluation in Higher Education* 24:4, 391–398. Table reproduced by permission of Taylor & Francis, Inc. http://www.tandf.co.uk/journals.

Bornman, Elirea. 1999. "Self-Image and Ethnic Identification in South Africa." *Journal of Social Psychology* 139:4, 411–425. Table reprinted with permission of the Helen Dwight Reid Educational Foundation. Published by Heldref Publications, 1319 Eighteenth St., NW, Washington, DC 20036–1802. Copyright © 1999.

Brock, Thomas, Isaac Kwakye, Judy C. Polyné, Lashawn Richburg-Hayes, David Seith, Alex Stepick, Carol Dutton Stepick, with Tara Cullen and Sarah Rich. 2004. "Welfare Reform in Miami: Implementation, Effects, and Experiences of Poor Families and Neighborhoods." New York: MDRC. Table used by permission of MDRC (www.mdrc.org).

Burnett, Derek M., Stephanie A. Kolakowsky-Hayner, Joy M. White, and David X. Cifu. 2002. "Impact of Minority Status Following Traumatic Spinal Cord Injury." *NeuroRehabilitation* 17, 187–194. Table reprinted with permission from IOS Press.

Chambers, Sharon M., James C. Hardy, Brenda J. Smith, and Sarah F. Sienty. 2003. "Personality Indicators and Emergency Permit Teachers' Willingness to Embrace Technology." *Journal of Instructional Psychology* 30:3, 185–188. Table published by permission of the *Journal of Instructional Psychology*.

Gfroerer, Kelly P., Coleman A. Gfroerer, William L. Curlette, JoAnna White, and Roy M. Kern. 2003. "Psychological Birth Order and the *Basis-A Inventory*." *Journal of Individual Psychology* 59:1, 30–41. Table used by permission of and copyright © 2003 by the University of Texas Press. All rights reserved.

Grosswald, Blanche. 2003. "Shift Work and Negative Work-to-Family Spillover." *Journal of Sociology and Social Welfare* 30:4, 31–56. Table used by permission of the *Journal of Sociology and Social Welfare*.

Hall-Elston, Claudia, and Larry C. Mullins. 1999. "Social Relationships, Emotional Closeness, and Loneliness Among Older Meal Program Participants." *Social Behavior and Personality* 27:5, 503–518. Table used by permission of *Social Behavior and Personality.*

Huff, Darrell. 1954. *How To Lie With Statistics.* New York: Norton.

Joshi, Anupama and Jennifer C. Ferris. 2002. "Causal Attributions Regarding Conflicts Between Friends in Middle Childhood. *Social Behavior and Personality* 30:1, 65–74. Table used by permission of *Social Behavior and Personality.*

Kakavoulis, Alexandros. 2001. "Family and Sex Education: A Survey of Parental Attitudes." *Sex Education* 1:2, 163–174. Table reproduced by permission of Taylor & Francis, Inc. http://www.tandf.co.uk/journals.

Kemple, James J. with Judith Scott-Clayton. 2004. "Career Academies: Impacts on Labor Market Outcomes and Educational Attainment." New York: MDRC. Table used by permission of MDRC (www.mdrc.org).

Looker, E.D. and Victor Thiessen. 1999. "Images of Work: Women's Work, Men's Work, Housework." *Canadian Journal of Sociology* 24:2, 225–254. Table used by permission of the *Canadian Journal of Sociology.*

Mayo, Joseph A. 2002. "Case-Based Instruction: A Technique for Increasing Conceptual Application in Introductory Psychology. *Journal of Constructivist Psychology* 15: 65–74.

Menet, Fiona, John Eakin, Michael Stuart, and Harry Rafferty. 2000. "Month of Birth and Effect on Literacy, Behaviour and Referral to Psychological Service." *Educational Psychology in Practice* 16:2, 225–234. Table reproduced by permission of Taylor & Francis, Inc. http://www.tandf.co.uk/journals.

Rovai, Alfred P. and Marcus D. Childress. 2002/2003. "Explaining & Predicting Resistance to Computer Anxiety Reduction among Teacher Education Students." *Journal of Research on Technology in Education* 35: 2, 226–235. Table reprinted with permission from the *Journal of Research on Technology in Education,* copyright © 2002/2003, ISTE (International Society for Technology in Education), 1.800.336.5191 (US & Canada) or 1.541.302.3777 (International), iste@iste.org, www.iste.org. All rights reserved.

Salka, William M. 2003. "Determinants of Countywide Voting Behavior on Environmental Ballot Measures: 1990–2000." *Rural Sociology* 68:2, 253–277. Table used with permission of the Rural Sociology Society.

Stein, Robert M. 1998. "Introduction: Early Voting." *Public Opinion Quarterly* 62:1, 57–69. Table used by permission of Oxford University Press.

Stevens, Daphne Pedersen, Gary Kiger, and Pamela J. Riley. "Coming Unglued? Workplace Characteristics, Work Satisfaction, and Family Cohesion." *Social Behavior and Personality* 30:3, 289–302. Table used by permission of *Social Behavior and Personality.*

Trudel, Gilles. 2002. "Sexuality and Marital Life: Results of a Survey." *Journal of Sex & Marital Therapy* 28: 229–249. Table Copyright © 2002 by Trudel and reproduced by permission of Taylor & Francis, Inc. http://www.taylorandfrancis.com.

Yoon, Jina S. 2002. "Teacher Characteristics as Predictors of Teacher-Student Relationships: Stress, Negative Affect, and Self-Efficacy." *Social Behavior and Personality* 30:5, 485–494. Table used by permission of *Social Behavior and Personality.*

FURTHER RESOURCES

Babbie, Earl. 2003. *The Practice of Social Research.* Tenth Edition. Belmont, CA: Wadsworth.

Campbell, Donald and Julian Stanley. 1963. *Experimental and Quasi-Experimental Designs for Research.* Boston: Hoghton Mifflin.

Miller, Delbert C. 1991. *Handbook of Research Design and Social Measurement.* 5th ed. Newbury Park, CA: Sage.

Nardi, Peter M. 2003. *Doing Survey Research: A Guide to Quantitative Methods.* Boston: Allyn & Bacon.

Neuman, W. Lawrence. 2003. *Social Research Methods: Qualitative and Quantitative Approaches.* Fifth Edition. Needham Heights, MA: Allyn & Bacon.

Norusis, Marija A. 2004. *SPSS 12.0 Guide to Data Analysis.* New York: Prentice Hall.

Phillips, John L. Jr. 2000. *How To Think About Statistics.* Sixth Edition. New York: Freeman.

WEB RESOURCES

Many Internet sites with statistical and research methods information can be found on the author's web page: http://pzacad.pitzer.edu/~pnardi/soc101links.html

INDEX

■ ■ ■ ■ ■ ▬▬▬▬▬▬▬▬▬▬▬▬▬▬▬▬▬▬▬▬▬▬▬▬▬▬▬▬▬▬▬▬

118